DARK ROAD

'Dark Road establishes Rankin as the fresh new voice
of Scottish theatre. With Thomson, he has produced an
unpretentious, honest evening's entertainment'
Evening News

'Excellent entertainment indeed' *Financial Times*

'Dark Road is a gripping and chilling piece of psychological
drama, paced expertly by its creators and brought to life
both by an accomplished cast and striking design'
Edinburgh Spotlight

'Utterly gripping, gritty and great entertainment, this
is a welcome and long overdue addition to the theatrical
thriller genre' *The Public Reviews*

'A creepily believable mixture of anger and geniality'
Guardian

'A great cast, a stunningly ambitious rotating pedestal of
sets designed by Francis O'Connor and a whodunit reveal
which is typically Rankin' *Independent*

'The psychological cat and mouse game . . . is top-notch
prime time stuff' *Herald*

'Dark Road teeters at that crossroads of modern era and
golden age, warning us that for all the material world
changes, human nature remains the same' *TV Bomb*

IAN RANKIN
MARK THOMSON
DARK ROAD

First published in Great Britain in 2014 by Orion Books,
an imprint of The Orion Publishing Group Ltd
Orion House, 5 Upper Saint Martin's Lane
London WC2H 9EA

An Hachette UK Company

1 3 5 7 9 10 8 6 4 2

A CIP catalogue record for this book is
available from the British Library.

ISBN (Hardback) 978 1 4091 5263 7
ISBN (Ebook) 978 1 4091 5265 1

Printed in Great Britain by Clays Ltd, St Ives plc

The Orion Publishing Group's policy is to use papers that
are natural, renewable and recyclable products and made from
wood grown in sustainable forests. The logging and manufacturing
processes are expected to conform to the environmental regulations
of the country of origin.

www.orionbooks.co.uk

DARK ROAD: A JOURNEY

As far as I remember, it started almost as a dare.

I've known Mark Thomson for years. He's a playwright and director as well as being Artistic Director of Edinburgh's Lyceum Theatre. There's a café near the theatre where we would rendezvous now and then for coffee and conversation. It was during one of these that we got talking about the popularity of crime. From the bestseller lists to our TV screens – fictional cops seem to be everywhere. But not on the contemporary stage.

'Is that because it can't be done?' Mark asked, throwing down the challenge. 'Why don't we find out?'

So we began work – tentatively – on a story that would become a script, and a script that would end up with a cast attached and the Lyceum booked for three weeks between September and October 2013.

I was very lucky to have Mark as a writing partner. Never having written for the stage before, there were obvious pitfalls I wasn't aware of at first. The cast couldn't be too unwieldy. Sudden shifts of scene or costume were problematic. Too many complicated props or effects and we'd be asking for trouble. Fortunately, Mark steered a clear course between these obstacles, and persuaded set designer Francis O'Connor to come up with a revolving stage that would speed up the action. We knew we wanted to put on a breathless thriller, one that would keep the audience on the edge of their seats. Francis helped make this possible.

Each day for me was full of fascinating new insights. I remember walking into the rehearsal studio and seeing architectural plans pinned to the wall, representing the revolving stage. Then a maquette of the same arrived. Actors were fitted for costumes. A table of props stood ready. Lighting designer Malcolm Rippeth arrived, as did composer Philip Pinsky. Assistant Director Jo Rush was by Mark's side throughout, as was Stage Manager Dan Travis – marking any changes to the script and timing each scene to the absolute second.

Then there were the actors. We knew we were asking a lot of Maureen Beattie – she appears in almost every scene. At the first and second read-throughs, there were questions to be answered as the cast started to get inside the heads of their characters. This process intensified once proper rehearsals got under way, and the complex choreography of each scene started to come alive, the actors adding nuance and texture. The main cast of eight began to gel, finding moments of humour, tension and tenderness in the script, so that the words began to live. It was a particular pleasure for me to meet Ron Donachie (Black Fergus in the play). Ron has played Rebus several times in BBC radio productions of my books. Then there was another face I recognised – Philip Whitchurch. Eventually it dawned on me – Phil had played a gangster in the TV adaptation of my novel *Doors Open*. A quality cast from top to bottom, hand-picked by Mark Thomson and ready for whatever challenges the production might throw at them.

I attended these rehearsals as often as I could, though the process by now belonged to the cast and crew rather than the writer. I was away on a book tour, however, when the production moved from the Lyceum's rehearsal studio across the street into the theatre proper. When I did finally manage a visit, I was overwhelmed once more. The set really was a thing of wonder, and the lights, music and visual effects seemed perfect. With the actors finally in their costumes, we could now see what the play would look like to an audience. Not that it was *quite* the finished article. After the first preview, Mark made a couple of tough but worthwhile decisions – one scene got the chop, and a tweak to the finale lessened the body count ever so slightly.

The result, on opening night, was a spine-tingling psychological thriller that kept the audience guessing, had them laughing out loud a few times (at the right places, thankfully), and made them jump and gasp a few times, too.

Mark and I had started out wanting to put a contemporary cop drama on stage, one set in the Edinburgh of the here and now, and a play that would prove popular, maybe enticing people away from their

TVs and sofas for a night so we could show them what the theatre can do.

We're delighted that so many people took the journey with us down this particular dark road. Just remember: that light in the distance may not be what you think . . .

Ian Rankin

DARK ROAD

CHARACTERS

Chief Superintendent Isobel McArthur   late forties, Scottish.
Former Chief Constable

Alexandra McArthur   twenty-one, Scottish

Alfred Chalmers   mid–late sixties

Detective Superintendent Frank Bowman   about fifty

Chief Constable Fergus McLintock (Black Fergus)
retired, about seventy, Scottish

Judith   a young female nurse in secure hospital, late twenties

Janice   a young female constable, early–mid twenties

Drew   a young male constable, mid–late twenties

Young Man   about twenty

Sarah McElhenney

Young Male Nurse

Act One

SCENE ONE

Dark. ISOBEL MCARTHUR's sitting room. Homely. Not ultra-modern. Not old-fashioned. Practical, but not furnished without thought and care. Sounds of sex infiltrate.

In front of the sofa a figure or shape of a person appears to be emerging from the floor. Lights crack out. Shouting, and ISOBEL revealed leaping off chair or sofa where she has been asleep. She stands panting. Very slowly and uncertainly she recovers, reflects, looks behind her. She is fully dressed in police uniform.

ALEXANDRA comes through. She is dressed in her nightwear.

ALEXANDRA   Mum? Mum? You OK?

ISOBEL   What?

ALEXANDRA   You OK?

ISOBEL   Yes?

ALEXANDRA   You sure?

ISOBEL   Yes. What time is it?

ALEXANDRA   Late.

ISOBEL   How late?

ALEXANDRA   Late-late.

ISOBEL   Right.

ALEXANDRA   Need anything?

ISOBEL   No, no, I'm fine. It's my thirtieth tomorrow,
              you know.

ALEXANDRA   Mum, you are young for your age but—

ISOBEL   In the force. Done my thirty. Means I can
              retire.

ALEXANDRA   Are you going to?

ISOBEL   Not tomorrow.

ALEXANDRA   Good.

ISOBEL   Is it?

ALEXANDRA   I don't know. Is it? *(Beat)* Go to bed. Maybe
              take your uniform off first.

ISOBEL   Good idea. Good night.

ALEXANDRA   *(Leaving)* You sure you're—

ISOBEL   Yes, yes, love you.

*ALEXANDRA exits. ISOBEL sits down. She opens a laptop
and ruffles a stack of A4 printed pages. The sound of
lovemaking again from the next room.*

SCENE TWO

*ISOBEL is in her office. There is the sound of people
offstage, laughter, talk. It is ISOBEL's thirtieth. She has
a drink in her hand. It's a bare office with some A4
achievement-type things. On one wall there is a board with
a mixture of people and cases that she hasn't solved. She
is glad to be away from the others. She bursts a balloon
with a letter-opener. She puts on the Stone Roses' 'Fool's
Gold' and looks out the window. FRANK enters.*

FRANK   Thirty years in the force and still no fucking
taste.

ISOBEL   Where were you?

FRANK   Sorry, got held up. Miss me?

ISOBEL   I told you I wanted you to be there.

FRANK   That might be the most sentimental thing you
have ever said to me.

ISOBEL   Piss off.

FRANK   That's my girl.

ISOBEL   Show some respect for your chief
superintendent.

FRANK   All right, boss. You got a drink in here?

ISOBEL   Sorry, only coffee.

FRANK   Of course.

ISOBEL   Know me. Party girl.

FRANK   Was a time.

ISOBEL   Long ago, Frank.

FRANK   Past doesn't just go; s'like carbon – it dates
you.

ISOBEL   Regular enemas do it for me – try it, Frank,
you might be less full of shit.

FRANK   That's my girl.

ISOBEL   Yeah, well.

FRANK   Look who the cat dragged in.

He opens the door. FERGUS enters.

ISOBEL   Fergus!

FERGUS   Yes.

ISOBEL   I'm . . . I'm . . .

FERGUS   And I thought I was the only one old enough
to keep forgetting my name.

ISOBEL   I'm so chuffed you're—

FERGUS   Of course I'd be here.

ISOBEL   That's great.

FERGUS   Can I sit down?

ISOBEL   Of course, just—

FERGUS   Yes, I know how to sit and can still spot a chair
          in a confined space: the wheels creak and clank
          but still turn.

FRANK   What do you think, Fergus?

FERGUS   She looks a million.

FRANK   But the grey?

ISOBEL   Thanks, Frank.

FERGUS   Tough, well-earned and a little bit sexy.

FRANK   Careful, can't say that nowadays.

ISOBEL   Yes he can. What are you doing? Not seen you
          for maybe three years.

FERGUS   I garden, I stalk my grandchildren and try
          and hammer the order and respect into them
          that their empowering, 'you're the centre of
          the universe' parents have failed to do. I wear
          out the hall rug with endless petty trips to the
          kitchen for tea, put things in the bin, tidy up,
          and then there's the increasing trips to the
          bathroom – hard to believe that night-time can
          bring on so much urine with so little drinking.
          So—

ISOBEL   That's an awful lot of information, Fergus.

FERGUS   So my point is, young Isobel—

ISOBEL   That now I've done my thirty and am able to
         get my pension, it's not all it's cracked up to be
         out there?

FRANK   She's sharp.

FERGUS   Course she's sharp. She's also a woman, and
         it's tough here.

ISOBEL   Now, Fergus, that is outright—

FERGUS   I don't care. I'm bloody fond of you and I'll say
         what I want – I'm sixty-eight and I don't give
         a shit. One of the benefits. Probably the only
         benefit.

FRANK   How's your sex life?

FERGUS   *(Glares)* My wife's in a wheelchair.

FRANK   Not all the time.

FERGUS   You've always been a wee bit sick, Frank,
         haven't you?

FRANK   *(Stands next to ISOBEL)* We are what God and
         Black Fergus made us. We are your spawn,
         Black Fergus. We are beautiful, sharp, going
         grey and sick. And we're yours.

They all laugh.

ISOBEL   Seven years out. You're proof there's life after
         being a cop. You're looking good.

FERGUS   No, I'm not. Did it bother you not getting
          the top job?

ISOBEL   Didn't get it – over.

FRANK   Still Queen of Police in Edinburgh!

ISOBEL   Yeah.

FERGUS   How's the wee one?

ISOBEL   She's twenty-one.

FERGUS   No she's not.

ISOBEL   She is. Final year at uni.

FERGUS   What's she doing there?

ISOBEL   Film and TV. Doing her final project. Wants
          to be Spielberg. Or a kind of documentary
          Spielberg.

FRANK   In the DNA: search for truth.

ISOBEL   Seeing you . . . You were a great boss, Fergus.
          I have everything to thank you for.

FERGUS   What am I supposed to do with that?

FRANK   Stick it up your jacksie and enjoy.

FERGUS   Listen, we're here to fix the shit when it hits
          the people. *(Beat)* For a wee moment there I
          actually forgot. Was still here, you know, doing
          it. Hang in there.

FRANK   Will do, sir.

FERGUS   I know you will. You've nothing else to do or
          live for.

FRANK   Cracker. Thanks.

ISOBEL   So much paperwork before I can get at any
          bad guys . . .

FRANK   Hey – be a chief super and say hello to a
          big desk of paperwork between you and being
          a cop.

ISOBEL   Broken record. I'm still a cop, Frank.

FRANK   I do it every day and I can touch it.

ISOBEL   I touch it.

FRANK   Course you do. It's under that paperweight.

ISOBEL   Don't start your real-police shit again. That
          really why you stayed a detective, so you could
          still feel the street, Frank?

FRANK   That's why.

ISOBEL   Sure.

FRANK   Absolutely.

ISOBEL   Whatever, I'm still doing it.

FRANK   Really, who with?

ISOBEL   That's crass.

FRANK   That's me. Still got the dirt and mess of the
          street on my shoes and in my mouth.

ISOBEL   Get a mouthwash and a shoe shine and do us
          all a—

FERGUS   Just like old times.

ISOBEL   I was the first female chief constable in
          Scotland. If I want to retire and go on
          supporting Alexandra, I thought I might write
          a book.

FRANK   What about?

ISOBEL   About me?

FRANK laughs.

ISOBEL   Thanks for that encouragement, Frank.

FRANK   Sorry, I didn't mean to . . . No, well I did. You're
          a cop, not a writer!

ISOBEL   Thought I wasn't a cop?

FRANK   Who'll buy it?

ISOBEL   It's not uninteresting, my job.

FRANK   Course not, but where's the headline? I just
          don't know if 'Scotland's First Female Chief
          Constable' is going to put you on the
          bestseller list.

ISOBEL   No, but Alfred Chalmers might.

Beat.

ISOBEL   It's just a thought.

FRANK   That's a bad thought.

ISOBEL   Maybe.

FRANK   That's a bad, bad thought. You put that
           thought out your head.

ISOBEL   I don't know how much longer I can keep going
           at this.

FRANK   Not good enough.

ISOBEL   It was twenty-five years—

FERGUS   —ago this October.

FRANK   You've really thought this out. Silver jubilee
           of his arrest. Fergus, you say something.

ISOBEL   It's a long time ago.

FRANK   So why drag him back up? Why drag those
           young women's bodies back up? Have you told
           their mothers?

ISOBEL   You're the first people I've told because I know
           it's your story too.

FRANK   It's not a fucking story, Isobel, it was a
           real-life nightmare and it was yesterday,
           I mean yesterday.

FERGUS   Have you spoken to him?

    Beat.

FRANK   For fuck's sake, Isobel, have you been speaking
         to that piece of—

ISOBEL   Not yet.

FRANK   Not yet?

ISOBEL   Not yet.

FRANK paces.

FERGUS   Is there something else, Isobel?

ISOBEL   What do you mean?

FERGUS   The book. The why.

ISOBEL   *(Beat)* I've always had . . . It unnerves me why
         I am so uncomfortable with his conviction
         twenty-five years on.

FRANK   Oh Jesus Christ.

FERGUS   Not the Lord, Frank.

FRANK   Sorry, Fergus.

ISOBEL   Why does it still bother me? Why can't I
         file it?

FERGUS   When we were searching for each one of those
         girls' bodies, placed in Chalmers' careful
         pattern, pulling legs out of trees, scraping
         heads out of rusting oil cans and reading
         'It's in the stars' scrawled in blood on their
         bellies, the cryptic clue that would lead to the

next part of the human jigsaw; and when we
saw that black ugly tar and diamanté jewels
where their young shining eyes once had been:
well, Isobel, we became participants in his foul
quest. He led and we had to dance, or we didn't
win. So if then, now, here, you might harbour
some doubt *(He physically winces)* about guilt,
whether it be his or even your own, like a
rattle, loose and unfixed at the back of your
head, then distrust it, because it's *his* pattern
that makes it.

FRANK   Too right. What he said.

ISOBEL *(To FRANK)* You're OK about it?

FRANK   Am I OK about him being locked up? You bet
your fucking granny's life I'm OK about it.

ISOBEL We only got him on the fourth – we didn't
prove the first three.

FRANK   So what?

ISOBEL You think that's satisfactory?

FRANK   It was twenty-five years ago.

ISOBEL That doesn't make it right.

FRANK   It doesn't make it wrong. We got the guy.

ISOBEL Did we?

FRANK   Please tell me this is a momentary and irrational burst of conscience. Or a moment of greed to sell your book.

ISOBEL   I don't know. I'm in the middle of it.

FRANK   Get out of the middle of it. Or you put us there too. You want that, Isobel? I don't want to be there. And neither does Fergus. We don't deserve it. You keep your eye on your job, do the paperwork, we stop the bad guys hurting and stealing and fucking up the good guys, or the OK-ish guys, or even the not so bad guys, and that's good, that's great, and it doesn't work perfectly but it's good. What you're doing, it's nothing. It's black. Isn't it, Black Fergus? Ask him? Isn't it? Oh fuck.

FRANK exits.

ISOBEL   I don't want to hurt you, Fergus. I've put in a request to see him. He might not agree anyway. Fergus, Chalmers was put away because of eighties forensic evidence that was creaky back then on the fourth victim. Nothing on the three other girls. He never cracked once. I'm not saying he didn't do it, he probably did, but . . .

FERGUS gets up with difficulty and in some pain.

FERGUS   The hunch of a police officer has become a
         playful element of fictional crime-solving. But
         all this paper piled up neatly, filed and stored,
         hasn't the weight of a copper's hunch. And
         I tell you, Isobel, the ugliness of that man,
         the deep, deep ugliness, was the nearest to
         pestilence I ever encountered. I know he did
         it, did all of them. You don't need a wedding
         ring to know you're loved, Isobel. Don't dirty
         yourself. Don't bring those girls up again.
         It won't clear it up. Sorry. Don't do it. Sorry.

FERGUS exits. ISOBEL walks to the door and calls through.

ISOBEL   Drew?

DREW   Ma'am?

ISOBEL   Come here a minute.

DREW enters, a bit worse for wear.

ISOBEL   Drew, can you do me a favour?

DREW   Anything, ma'am, especially today.

ISOBEL   Thank you. I'd like you to arrange to get all
         the files on a closed case sent over.

DREW   OK.

ISOBEL   *(Writing)* Details here.

DREW   Was that Black Fergus just here?

ISOBEL   Yes, that was him.

DREW   Man's a legend.

ISOBEL   Yes, he is. Here.

She hands him the piece of paper. He looks at it and looks at her. She nods.

ISOBEL   Make sure you get everything. The cassettes.
            Everything.

DREW   Cassettes? Oh yeah. Any reason?

Beat. DREW starts to go.

ISOBEL   Drew, I'd appreciate it if you kept this to
            yourself. Saves any silly questions. You know,
            like the one you just asked.

DREW   Gotcha, ma'am.

ISOBEL   And Drew, I'm very glad you won Tail on the
            Donkey.

DREW   Me too. It was a good moment for me.

ISOBEL   More to come, I'm sure.

DREW   I hope so.

DREW exits. ISOBEL phones on her mobile.

ISOBEL   Hello. *(Beat)* It's Chief Superintendent
          Isobel McArthur here. Yes, I e-mailed you
          about Alfred Chalmers. Have you had any
          response from him? *(Beat)* Yes, I'm sure he was
          surprised. *(Beat)* No, it's not an official request
          and really I'm . . . well, it's not that I definitely
          want to see him. I wanted to be clear on his
          position. *(Beat)* He's considering it. Right.
          Right. *(Beat)* No, there's no developments, just
          . . . let me know. Thanks. *(Beat)* Thank you.
          Goodbye.

A screech of someone from the party next door.

SCENE THREE

ALEXANDRA at home on the phone, in the middle of a conversation.

ALEXANDRA   Yes. *(Beat)* Yes, that's right. *(Beat)* I'm not fearless; I just want what I do to make a difference, and the more we talk, the more I think we could really do something here. I mean, it's complicated, and people are going to be uncomfortable, but that doesn't mean we should shy away from it, does it? *(Beat. Laughs)* Yes, and it started with a tweet. Sounds like a bad song. How random is this. Well, maybe it's not. *(Beat)* Thanks, I didn't think anyone would read my reviews, but hey, I've got three hundred and sixty-three followers – and you, of course. *(Beat)* But I don't want to be a critic. I want to make TV that is meaningful, that surprises you with how it looks and acts on you, but I really want it to mean something when every time I turn on the—

ISOBEL enters. She has been cycling, sweaty. Helmet off.

ALEXANDRA   Sorry, got to go. *(Beat)* I know. It's just I feel we're just getting started and . . . *(Beat)*

OK. OK. Bye. *(Hangs up)* Hello. How many miles?

ISOBEL   Twenty.

ALEXANDRA   Slouch.

ISOBEL   I'm getting old.

ALEXANDRA   Keep pedalling.

ISOBEL   The great race you always lose in the end.

ALEXANDRA   Pedal pedal.

ISOBEL   That him from the other night?

ALEXANDRA   No.

ISOBEL   He was a bit short.

ALEXANDRA   For you?

ISOBEL   For you!

ALEXANDRA   Is this official questioning?

ISOBEL   OK. Is that short reply because it's an important guy or a very very *un*important guy?

ALEXANDRA   You're the cop.

ISOBEL   Yes, I am. How's the big project going?

ALEXANDRA   Makes it sound a little like a primary school insect-collecting trip.

ISOBEL   Sorry, didn't mean that. Bad mum.

23

ALEXANDRA   Yes, bad mum. If you want to know, I have
            started on something for my final project.
            It's edgy and I'm working with this person
            who I think could really open things up
            for me.

ISOBEL   That's fantastic.

ALEXANDRA   I know, I know. When you think someone's
            innocent or you get, you know, your cop
            hunch, you have to follow it, don't you?

ISOBEL   The only thing I have to follow is the law.

ALEXANDRA   I suppose that's the difference between art
            and police work. The truth lives behind the
            eyes of facts.

ISOBEL   That's good – you should use that in—

ALEXANDRA   Mum, you're being—

ISOBEL   I'm not condescending. I like it.

ALEXANDRA   Yeah? Should I write it down?

ISOBEL   Yes!

ALEXANDRA   What was it I said again?

ISOBEL   Now *my* mother if she heard you say that
            would say it must have been a lie.

ALEXANDRA   'The truth lives behind the eyes of facts.'
            Hmm.

ISOBEL   I have a fresh lasagne.

ALEXANDRA   Fresh from Tesco?

ISOBEL   Yes, I—

ALEXANDRA   Going out.

ISOBEL   Oh. Fine.

ALEXANDRA   Sorry.

ISOBEL   Is it him from last week, or someone else?

ALEXANDRA   It's Lilly and Mary, actually.

ISOBEL   Oh, OK.

ALEXANDRA   If that's OK with you.

ISOBEL   Fine, so probably alone, then?

ALEXANDRA   What?

ISOBEL   When you come back.

ALEXANDRA   Yes, probably.

ISOBEL   OK.

ALEXANDRA   There's loads of fat in lasagne.

ISOBEL   Do you think I'm getting fat?

ALEXANDRA   Yes.

ISOBEL   Oh.

ALEXANDRA   Sorry, was that too blunt?

ISOBEL   I can hardly complain.

ALEXANDRA   No, you can't.

ISOBEL   I'll save you some.

ALEXANDRA   Thanks.

ISOBEL   I got some green stuff to go with it.

ALEXANDRA   Well done.

ALEXANDRA takes up her iPad and notes and is about to head to her bedroom.

ISOBEL   Do I get an invite to the premiere?

ALEXANDRA   Of course you do.

ISOBEL   Anything wrong?

ALEXANDRA   No. I've made a breakthrough with this person and he's kind of the inspiration. My head is like jangling with ideas and images when I speak to him and I think there's a story there, it means something.

ISOBEL   Sounds great.

ALEXANDRA   This is my thing and I want you to support me in it.

ISOBEL   Of course I will.

ALEXANDRA   You were Scotland's first female chief constable and I want to make a mark too.

ISOBEL   Just being you.

ALEXANDRA   Yes, but apart from the 'mother-love you're special whatever'. I can do things.

ISOBEL   I know.

ALEXANDRA   OK.

ISOBEL   I'm sweaty.

ALEXANDRA   Sorry about the lasagne.

ISOBEL   Sorry I'm fat.

ALEXANDRA   You're not.

ALEXANDRA exits. ISOBEL takes out a pile of cassettes, files, etc. It is CHALMERS' case files, photographs. ALEXANDRA comes back through. ISOBEL quickly packs them away.

ALEXANDRA   Just heading out. Now who's being secretive?

ISOBEL   Sorry.

ALEXANDRA   What's the matter, Mum?

ISOBEL   Nothing.

ALEXANDRA   Mum?

ISOBEL   I'm thinking of writing a book.

ALEXANDRA   Great!

ISOBEL   If I retire, maybe it's something that could bring a little extra money in.

ALEXANDRA   Great idea.

ISOBEL   Maybe.

ALEXANDRA   Not to be disrespectful, but why do you
             think a book would sell?

ISOBEL   First female chief constable in Scotland.

ALEXANDRA   OK, that's a newspaper article.

ISOBEL   Thanks.

ALEXANDRA   Just saying.

ISOBEL   Some interesting cases.

ALEXANDRA   *(Pointing to briefcase)* Like in there?

ISOBEL   Mm-hm.

ALEXANDRA   OK. Great.

ISOBEL   Are you OK with that?

ALEXANDRA   Am I in your book?

ISOBEL   Not written it yet, but no, it'll be purely
             police work.

ALEXANDRA   Well if I'm not in it, I've lost interest
             already. Good luck.

ISOBEL   Really?

ALEXANDRA   Got to go, Mum.

ISOBEL   Thanks.

ALEXANDRA   Right. Bye.

ISOBEL   Bye.

ALEXANDRA exits. ISOBEL takes a bunch of files including clippings, photographs, etc., and spreads them over the floor and table. They take over the room, with each place having its own particular zone: victims' photographs, press clippings, reports, etc.

ISOBEL   Lorraine. Rebecca. Lisa. Sarah. Dear God. There you are. Still there. Still gone.

She finally takes a cassette recorder out of her bag and puts it down, places one of the cassettes inside, hesitates, presses play. Nothing happens. She gets prickly skin and itches, rubs at her neck and arms. She picks up photographs of the four victims. She places them side by side.

ISOBEL   Sarah. Welcome home, Sarah. It's all done. It's only stories now. I won't disturb you, I hope.

CHALMERS   *(Voice from cassette. He has a cold and sniffs throughout)* Here we are again.

ISOBEL starts, swung back twenty years by the voice.

CHALMERS   *(Voice from cassette)* Have you found him yet?

ISOBEL   *(Voice from cassette)* Have we found who?

CHALMERS   *(Voice from cassette)* The man who killed
                those girls.

FRANK   *(Voice from cassette)* Oh yeah, we found him.

ISOBEL   *(Voice from cassette)* Interview begins eight
                thirty a.m. November the sixth, 1988.
                Present in the room are Alfred Chalmers,
                Chief Superintendent Fergus McLintock,
                Detective Inspector Frank Bowman and
                Detective Constable Isobel McArthur.

FERGUS   *(Voice from cassette)* When did you meet
                Lorraine Robertson?

CHALMERS   *(Voice from cassette)* I didn't. Have you got a
                tissue or something?

FERGUS   *(Voice from cassette)* But you were an orderly
                at the hospital where Miss Robertson was
                admitted for a termination.

CHALMERS   *(Voice from cassette)* There are many women
                come and go there, you should know that.

FERGUS   *(Voice from cassette)* And do you remember
                when you met Rebecca Telford?

CHALMERS   *(Voice from cassette)* No.

FERGUS   *(Voice from cassette)* Lisa Brown?

CHALMERS   *(Voice from cassette)* No.

FERGUS   *(Voice from cassette)* Sarah McElhenney?

CHALMERS   *(Voice from cassette)* Yes.

FERGUS   *(Voice from cassette)* When was that?

CHALMERS   *(Voice from cassette)* Early September, I think it was. You can check – the hospital will keep records.

FRANK   *(Voice from cassette)* Well fuck me, you're a real helpful c—

CHALMERS   *(Voice from cassette)* I really need something for my nose, could you . . .

ISOBEL   *(Voice from cassette)* Here.

CHALMERS   *(Voice from cassette)* Thank you.

FERGUS   *(Voice from cassette)* Did she stick in your mind?

CHALMERS   *(Voice from cassette)* Sorry.

FERGUS   *(Voice from cassette)* Well, you've forgotten about the others. What made Sarah stand out, do you think?

CHALMERS   *(Voice from cassette)* Sarah's the name of my daughter.

FERGUS   *(Voice from cassette)* These records at the hospital – do you have access to them?

CHALMERS   *(Voice from cassette)* No, only medical staff.

FERGUS   *(Voice from cassette)* Would it be possible for
                you to see them? Their addresses?

CHALMERS   *(Voice from cassette)* I don't know, because I
                never tried.

ISOBEL   *(Voice from cassette)* What would you do if
                your Sarah turned up for an abortion at the
                hospital?

CHALMERS   *(Voice from cassette)* Would never happen,
                not my Sarah.

ISOBEL   *(Voice from cassette)* How do you know?

CHALMERS   *(Voice from cassette)* They came into
                the hospital like they were making a
                withdrawal from their bank.

ISOBEL   *(Voice from cassette)* What if they were
                raped?

CHALMERS   *(Voice from cassette)* They weren't.

ISOBEL   *(Voice from cassette)* Weren't they?

CHALMERS   *(Voice from cassette)* Well how would I know?

FRANK   *(Voice from cassette)* Good question, Alfred.

CHALMERS   *(Voice from cassette)* If I say I know them,
                you do your evil maths and use it on me. I
                say I don't know them and you say I must.
                You've decided, because you want to win. I
                don't like what those girls did, no, I don't.
                And do you know why? Because

I think human life is sacred. Sacred. Now
do your maths.

FRANK   *(Voice from cassette)* You're not maths,
Chalmers. You're the mess that happens
before maths.

CHALMERS   *(Voice from cassette)* I didn't kill those girls.

ISOBEL   *(Voice from cassette)* Even though they killed
their babies?

CHALMERS   *(Voice from cassette)* That's right, provocative
Isobel.

FRANK   *(Voice from cassette)* Good name,
'Provocative Isobel'.

CHALMERS   *(Voice from cassette suddenly loud, wild)*
You slimy fucking prick Frank flipping
your stupid dumb-boy words like you mean
something. You think you're funny but
God help you if you ever lose the uniform
because

ALEXANDRA enters unnoticed.

Frank you are a cunt because you have
nothing on me and the reason you have
nothing on me is because there is nothing
to have on me because I didn't do it. *(Calmer
now)* And you, Isobel, you want it to be me
too much. And that is not right—

ISOBEL notices ALEXANDRA. She puts off the cassette.

ALEXANDRA   Sorry, forgot my purse, I—

ISOBEL   Sorry, it's an old case I'm—

ALEXANDRA   For your book?

ISOBEL   Yes, yes, for the book. Maybe, I don't know.

ALEXANDRA   *(Laughs)* You don't know?

ISOBEL   Still thinking.

ALEXANDRA   You can probably get something for that on eBay, you know.

ISOBEL   Sorry? Oh, OK, yes. Look, have a nice night.

ALEXANDRA picks up her purse. ISOBEL gathers up the files.

ISOBEL   Sorry about . . .

ALEXANDRA   Night.

ISOBEL   Night. Be safe.

ALEXANDRA   *(Laughs)* I'm always safe. My mother's chief of police!

ALEXANDRA exits. ISOBEL drops one of the photos on the floor. She looks at it. Uneasily she picks it up.

ISOBEL   Sarah. Sarah.

Blackout.

SCENE FOUR

Midnight. Living room. There is the intermittent sound of noisy sex coming from off. Phone rings. A tired ISOBEL enters, drags herself to find the phone. Answers.

ISOBEL   Hello. *(Pause)* Hello.

She puts the phone down. She hears the sex. She pours herself a whisky. She picks a file off the floor, places another cassette in the player and reads as she listens.

CHALMERS   *(Voice from the cassette, sounding tired)*
... whether the most important thing is what you do or maybe *why* you do what you do. You're keen, aren't you, Isobel. Keen to get on. The guys here see something in you, maybe something of the *man.*

FRANK   *(Voice from the cassette)* More of a man than you.

CHALMERS   *(Voice from the cassette)* Or maybe they just want to have you.

FERGUS   *(Voice from the cassette)* Now, now, Alfred.

CHALMERS   *(Voice from the cassette)* I don't want you to think I've anything against women ...

FRANK   *(Voice from the cassette)* He's a stand-up!

CHALMERS   *(Voice from the cassette)* . . . but it must be
               hard with all these men and you must have
               to try that bit harder.

ISOBEL   *(Voice from the cassette)* Is that wrong?

CHALMERS   *(Voice from the cassette)* But you're so
               desperate to make your mark that you
               might just stare and stare till you see what
               you want to see. You might just push and
               push till you get what you think you want
               to get. And that's where it stops being
               clean.

ISOBEL   *(Voice from the cassette)* Can't the truth be
               messy?

CHALMERS   *(Voice from the cassette)* The truth *is* messy
               enough without your mess stuck all over
               it. Me connected with those women – a
               fact and a truth you are twisting to death
               to create the illusion that will gain you
               something, selfish girl. Meanwhile, the guys
               slip secret looks at you and get hard-ons—

*ISOBEL hears the sex get louder and turns up the volume
almost pettily.*

FERGUS   *(Voice from the cassette)* What do you know
               about the constellations?

CHALMERS   *(Voice from the cassette)* I'm Gemini. What
            are you?

FERGUS   *(Voice from the cassette)* 'It's in the stars' and
            'Look up'. What do you think that means?
            Why write that?

CHALMERS   *(Voice from the cassette)* No idea. Wrote that
            on them, did he?

ISOBEL   *(Voice from the cassette)* In blood on their
            stomachs. After we found your third victim,
            Lisa, we saw your pattern. The constellation
            of Cassiopeia: the Vain Queen. So we knew
            where the next victim would be found.

FRANK   *(Voice from the cassette)* Star 1, Lorraine
            Robertson, in an oil drum near the Junction
            of Ferry Road and Granton; Star 2, Rebecca
            Telford, in a tree under the Dean Bridge;
            Star 3, Lisa Brown, hanging on the railings
            around the Dugald Stewart Monument on
            Calton Hill; Star 4, not in pattern, hidden
            under the floorboards like a guilty secret.

CHALMERS   *(Voice from the cassette)* I don't know
            anything about stars!

FERGUS   *(Voice from the cassette)* What went wrong
            with Sarah, Alfred? Wasn't found where
            she should have been. Panic? And there are
            five stars in that constellation. That'll never
            happen now, will it?

CHALMERS *(Voice from the cassette)* Piss off, Fergus. Your compass is broke and your science compromised. It found me and it lied. Because you invented this, not me. And you did this, not me.

ALEXANDRA enters. She is drunk and with a dressing gown wrapped around her.

ALEXANDRA Can you turn that down?

ISOBEL turns it off.

ISOBEL Can you?

ALEXANDRA Fuck off.

ISOBEL I'll turn it down.

ALEXANDRA What are you listening to him for?

ISOBEL Him?

ALEXANDRA It's him, isn't it? Chalmers.

ISOBEL How did you know it was—

ALEXANDRA Chalmers? Twenty-fifth anniversary of his arrest. You're writing a book. 'Biggest fish I ever caught.' You. Him.

ISOBEL My book is of no interest to any publisher unless he's in it.

ALEXANDRA He's your trophy serial killer.

ISOBEL   Maybe.

ALEXANDRA   Do you need to write a book?

ISOBEL   I want to write it.

ALEXANDRA   OK.

ISOBEL   Do you need to do your project?

ALEXANDRA   Good to talk.

ISOBEL   It's late to talk.

ALEXANDRA   Maybe it is.

ISOBEL   I meant late at night.

ALEXANDRA   Maybe it all started with him? *(Indicates tape recorder)*

ISOBEL   What did?

ALEXANDRA   I don't know. It.

ISOBEL   Honestly, Alex, you wear me out with your riddles.

A YOUNG MAN in boxers enters.

YOUNG MAN   You coming back, student Alex?

ALEXANDRA   Just wait in the bedroom.

YOUNG MAN   Cause my cock's ready for round two.
              (Sees ISOBEL) Oh, hello, Mum. Didn't know
              Mum was home. Oops.

ISOBEL   I'm not your mother. Just pretend I'm not
                here, why don't you.

ALEXANDRA   I didn't need to pretend. *(To YOUNG MAN)*
                Come on, Muhammad Ali. Let's see what
                you've got left.

*ALEXANDRA and YOUNG MAN exit. ISOBEL pours another
whisky. Throb of dance music from the next room. She
picks up files again, takes a laptop out and prepares to
write. She fast-forwards the cassette.*

ISOBEL   *(Voice from cassette)* . . . seventh interview
                with Alfred Chalmers. Date: November
                the nineteenth, 1988. Time: eight thirty-
                five p.m. Present: Detective Inspector
                Frank Bowman and Detective Constable
                Isobel McArthur. Where were you on the
                night of September the seventeenth? *(No
                response)* Records show you worked at the
                Royal Infirmary and finished your shift at
                seven p.m. that evening. Where did you go
                afterwards? *(No response)* Why did you put
                Sarah's body under her floorboards and
                not place it in public like the others? *(No
                response)*

ISOBEL   *(Looking at photographs)* Why put her in
                her own house? Why change the rules?
                Why was a strand of her clothing found on
                yours? How did that happen, Alfred?

FRANK   *(Voice from cassette)* It was clever what you did: you got the headlines just like you wanted, so now you can tell us the grand plan.

ISOBEL   *(Voice from cassette)* So they were all unemployed, they all had terminations. Am I being obvious, or is it just as simple as it seems?

ISOBEL   *(Shouting over the last bit of cassette dialogue)* Why did you change the rules? What happened? What—

CHALMERS *(Shouting from cassette at live ISOBEL)* Why can't you think up some original questions after twenty-five bloody years? Do I need to listen to all this shit again?

ISOBEL   You never answered the questions.

CHALMERS *(Voice from cassette)* You weren't clever enough to be rewarded with them.

ISOBEL   So what did those women do to be rewarded by you?

CHALMERS *(Voice from cassette)* Stinking wasters. Do-nothingers, breed in bed and flush the consequences down the plug hole.

ISOBEL   You never put Sarah, your fourth, in the constellation. Why?

At this point CHALMERS is revealed stirring a large saucepan full of tar.

CHALMERS   Look, I'm a bit busy right now: got to get this finished. No idea how my arm aches. Think stirring tar's easy? It's not. Got machines in builders'—

ISOBEL   Why not just kill them? Why hide her when you wanted the bodies to be found?

CHALMERS   Because it shone a light.

ISOBEL   On what? Why?

CHALMERS   On them. Creepy-crawlies. *(Giggles)*

ISOBEL   Did you watch them before you killed them?

CHALMERS   Of course. I am nothing if not thorough. If a job's worth doing . . .

ISOBEL   So you found out their addresses from the hospital records, you stalked them . . .

CHALMERS   Now, now, 'stalked' is a bit judgemental.

ISOBEL   And then when you felt safe, you murdered them.

CHALMERS   You think a woman can't stand up for herself, Constable Isobel?

ISOBEL   I'm a chief superintendent now.

CHALMERS   So you're better than that Constable Isobel back then?

ISOBEL   *(Voice from cassette)* Yes, Isobel, I think that's a bit much.

FRANK   *(Voice from cassette)* Bloody good copper you were too, Isobel, before you decided paperwork was your thing.

ISOBEL   Strategy, Frank. No strategy and we're all headless chickens.

FRANK   *(Voice from cassette)* You turned your back on the real work, dealing with people like him!

CHALMERS   He's got a point. I mean, you did catch me.

CHALMERS   *(Voice from cassette)* She caught the wrong person!

ISOBEL   *(Voice from cassette)* I caught the right person!

CHALMERS   Can I just get on with this, get it done and get some peace?

ISOBEL   OK, what's peace for you? What peace do you get when that girl stops breathing? What stops rattling in your head?

CHALMERS   Interference. White noise. All they are.

FRANK   *(Voice from cassette)* Can I hear someone fucking?

43

ISOBEL   Did something interrupt you taking her
              body out like the others?

CHALMERS   *(Voice from cassette)* Heard it all. She asked
              me that twenty-five years ago.

ISOBEL   *(Voice from cassette)* I did, actually.

FRANK   *(Voice from cassette)* I can definitely hear
              someone fucking. Isobel, is there someone
              having sex in the next room?

ISOBEL   Alexandra.

FRANK   *(Voice from cassette)* She's not even born yet.

ISOBEL   She is now. She's with Muhammad.

FRANK   *(Voice from cassette)* She's with a black guy?
              In Edinburgh? Fuck.

ISOBEL   No, not— shut up, Frank! What did the
              constellation mean? Cassiopeia?

CHALMERS   The Vain Queen.

ISOBEL   Yes.

CHALMERS   Can't help you.

ISOBEL   Why dump Sarah's body under the
              floorboards? It doesn't make sense.

CHALMERS   No, it doesn't, does it? This is disgusting.
              I shouldn't be doing this!

ISOBEL   So why are you?

CHALMERS   You're making me do it.

FRANK   *(Voice from cassette)* A black guy?

ISOBEL   But why?

CHALMERS   *(Finding a knife in his hand)* Have to do . . .
            what comes next.

ISOBEL   *(Voice from cassette)* Don't let him escape!

ISOBEL   Stop! Stop now!

CHALMERS   You can't stop me. It's already happened.

*The image of a person with a fox's head appears either
somewhere in the room or at the window of the house.
It is a bloody and disfigured mess with red eyes. Sex noises
a bit more focal. CHALMERS disappears/exits. Screams off.
ISOBEL sees FOXHEAD. Noise of sex from off suggesting
a move to climax at the end of dialogue.*

ISOBEL   What?

ISOBEL   *(Voice from cassette)* What is it? Have you let
            him go?

ISOBEL   Frank, there's something here with me, and
            it's not Chalmers.

ISOBEL	CHALMERS	FRANK
I am trying to make sense of this and I am facing up to the possibility . . .	Let me go! Let me go! You got the wrong man you fucking idiots. Let me go!	Shut up, you woman killer you scum.

FRANK   Those girls had nothing, and you took even that away from them.

CHALMERS   I didn't kill her. It wasn't me!

ISOBEL	CHALMERS	FRANK
No, I can't do this. We did it, we solved it, it's done – so why does it rattle about? Is it the book? Is it retiring?	It wasn't me. Invented me! Invented all this! All of it!	Come on, Isobel. Man up so those poor girls' mums and dads can sleep at night without – having their fucking daughters' tarred spangled faces screaming through their nightmares.

CHALMERS   It's all invented!

ISOBEL   Oh God. I don't want this back in my head
            again.

*FOXHEAD makes noise as if alert to ISOBEL. Will it attack
or run? It holds a finger up, points at her, puts finger to
its lips (or thereabouts) and goes as ALEXANDRA and the
YOUNG MAN climax.*

SCENE FIVE

FRANK, in ISOBEL's office. Sitting around waiting. JANICE enters. She has some papers, puts them on ISOBEL's desk. FRANK picks them up.

FRANK   I'm waiting. For the chief.

JANICE   Is she expecting you?

FRANK   No.

JANICE   Do you want me to get Jenny? She's got her diary.

FRANK   No, Jenny can stand down for the moment.

JANICE   OK.

FRANK   You like your job?

JANICE   Yes, sir.

FRANK   Good, good. You like working for the chief?

JANICE   Yes, she's great.

FRANK   Yes, she is.

JANICE   Anything I can get you?

FRANK   Have you got any more of that stuff on Chalmers she's been asking for?

JANICE   No, she's got it all. There's nothing more.
         Are we thinking of reopening that case, sir?

FRANK   Over my dead body.

JANICE   So why—

ISOBEL enters.

ISOBEL   Janice.

JANICE   Ma'am.

ISOBEL   Aha! Frank, I don't have you in my diary.

FRANK   *(To JANICE)* Janice, can you speak to Jenny
         about this, because if the chief super doesn't
         have me in her diary and I'm running CID,
         then the consequences could be disastrous.

ISOBEL   You can go now, Janice.

JANICE   Thanks, ma'am.

FRANK   And tell Jenny, Janice, that I'll have a word
         before I go.

JANICE exits.

ISOBEL   You're not funny.

FRANK   Well I am a bit.

ISOBEL   She's good, and your games mess with her
         head.

FRANK   If she's that good, she can deal with it.

ISOBEL   And there is no CID any more.

FRANK   Words, Isobel, words.

ISOBEL   God, this is endless.

FRANK   You must love your job.

ISOBEL   I do love my job.

FRANK   I'd hate your job. Your job doesn't let you do
         what you wanted to do when you signed up.

ISOBEL   Yes it does.

FRANK   No it doesn't.

ISOBEL   Do you need something? We'll be seeing each
         other at our Thursday morning briefing.

FRANK   Our chat stayed with me. Maybe even worried
         me a bit.

ISOBEL   You don't need to worry.

FRANK   Just strikes me as odd when you've got all
         this stuff to deal with and you're asking your
         protégé for files from a case that's closed and
         twenty-five years old. Because I know what
         I'm doing, Isobel. I'm dealing with the bad
         stuff right now and also getting ready for the
         next thing, so despite being – and I know I
         may be called this, though never to my face –
         a dinosaur, I am at least forward-thinking in
         that respect.

ISOBEL   Who said I've been looking at files?

FRANK   A little bird told me.

ISOBEL   Don't stalk me.

FRANK   I'm not. But you're not alone with this, and
you start dabbling then your fingers are going
to touch me. Actually, that's not an all that
unpleasant image.

ISOBEL   Nothing will interfere with my work.

FRANK   You sure?

ISOBEL   Don't fucking question me, Frank!

FRANK   God, you're sexy.

ISOBEL   You are in my office.

FRANK   *(Beat)* You sleeping OK?

ISOBEL   No, probably not.

FRANK   That's the start.

ISOBEL   If there's something to fix, is that wrong?

FRANK   *(Shouting)* There's nothing to fix.

ISOBEL   Maybe.

FRANK   Fuck 'maybe'. There's nothing to fix.

ISOBEL   Then why get so worked up?

FRANK   Because he messed us up then and he can do
it again.

ISOBEL   He's inside.

FRANK   He's a virus – he's already out. You name him
          and he's out and he's in me and you and in
          Fergus.

ISOBEL   That's rubbish – you're inventing him as
          something—

FRANK   I'm calling it like it is.

ISOBEL   There's nothing he can do to us.

FRANK   Fergus had a stroke.

ISOBEL   When?

FRANK   Last night.

ISOBEL   Why? I mean, why didn't you tell me when you
          came in, instead of . . . instead of—

FRANK   Because I needed to talk a bit and I thought it
          might be you could—

ISOBEL   You know what he means to me.

FRANK   I don't know. What *does* he mean to you?

ISOBEL   How fucking dare you ask me that?

FRANK   Because I don't think you bringing all this up
          again is exactly the act of a friend, or even in
          fact a colleague.

ISOBEL   You've no right to say this to me.

FRANK   Then who has? We were together then, in bed and at work.

ISOBEL   That's in the past, Frank.

FRANK   Can't you remember what it was like?

ISOBEL   The sex?

FRANK   What? No, not the sex. Though that too. That was then too. That time when we were investigating *him* and then when we got him. It got under our fingernails, it got up our nostrils; when I shat, I felt the worst of him go right through me. The universe is all dead-blood black and scattered with girls with no eyes. I wish we'd done him in and maybe that would have drawn a line.

ISOBEL   A line under what?

FRANK   Under *him*.

ISOBEL   I don't think I ever have.

FRANK   And now you're writing a book.

ISOBEL   It's not about the book.

FRANK   Alexandra's fees, is it?

ISOBEL   It's about me.

FRANK   You going to see him? *(Beat)* You've already seen him.

ISOBEL   No.

FRANK   He wouldn't see you?

ISOBEL   He's agreed to meet.

FRANK   What does he want?

ISOBEL   It's me wants to see him. *I* want something.

FRANK   He wants something. If he's meeting you, he
        wants something.

ISOBEL   I'll give him a chance to talk.

FRANK   He had his chance. Why let him talk – people
        might end up listening. *Think!*

ISOBEL   I'm going on a hunch.

FRANK   That a cop hunch or a misplaced conscience
        hunch?

ISOBEL   I'm going on a hunch that something isn't –
        wasn't right.

FRANK   Fuck your hunch. Put it away.

ISOBEL   I can't – I don't have a choice.

FRANK   Of course you have a choice. You've got a brain,
        use it. You forgotten everything?

ISOBEL   No, I thought I could, but I can't, and
        everything – me thinking about retiring, the
        twenty-fifth anniversary of his arrest – it's like
        the planets are all aligning.

FRANK   Bullshit! Bullshit, Isobel. Just bullshit! No,
          no, no – the only alignments were the ones he
          made when he placed those girls' bodies all
          over this city and then razored what he did
          here. *(Taps his forehead)*

ISOBEL   And all that anger and pain, Frank, if it was
          so clear, how come we never got any evidence
          about the first three?

FRANK   Because he was clever.

ISOBEL   And we weren't?

FRANK   The fibre from her coat was on his jacket.

ISOBEL   For the fourth. For Sarah.

FRANK   For the fourth, Sarah, yeah, and he was the
          only fucking human being alive that knew all
          those four girls. Now tell me what your hunch
          said then and what it says now.

ISOBEL   Maybe he'll tell me the truth and I'll write it
          and we can all get clean.

FRANK   I don't need to, I'm OK with being dirty. It goes
          with the job. Man up, Isobel.

ISOBEL   Spoken like a—

FRANK   True friend.

ISOBEL   I can't let it go. I'm scared!

FRANK   No wonder. Jesus Christ, no wonder. Do you
        care for your book or your conscience more
        than me, more than Black Fergus?

ISOBEL Yes.

DREW enters. Beat.

DREW   Just a signature. Jenny says you have
        Strathclyde at the desk, he's on his way up.

ISOBEL Not Strathclyde now; the Chief Constable of
        Scot—

DREW   Sorry, ma'am.

ISOBEL So was I.

DREW exits.

FRANK   He can't speak much, but he's stable. At the
        Royal Infirmary. Ward 7 on the east wing if you
        want to visit him.

ISOBEL Of course I want to visit him.

FRANK   I'm sure he'll be glad to see you, even though
        last time you . . . *You're* scared? You scare the
        fuck out of me, Isobel.

*FRANK exits. ISOBEL sits. Picks up a cup and smashes it.
JANICE re-enters.*

ISOBEL   Just a mug, Janice.

JANICE   Oh, right.

ISOBEL   It deserved it.

JANICE   *(Beat then)* I thought we just arrested people. Didn't think we carried out sentences.

ISOBEL   That mug was never going to be any good, Constable Harker, but technically of course you are right.

JANICE   I understand.

ISOBEL   Do you? Do I?

JANICE   Shall I get rid of the evidence?

ISOBEL   That would be lovely.

JANICE picks up the pieces.

ISOBEL   Do you want to be me, Janice?

JANICE   I want to be me, ma'am.

ISOBEL   That's a good answer. I have a daughter couple of years younger than you.

JANICE   Don't be surprised if she doesn't want to be you either.

ISOBEL   No. Why does nobody want to be me? What's wrong with me?

JANICE   You're great, ma'am. Shall I dispose of the . . .
         er, the . . .

ISOBEL   Quietly, where no one can find it.

JANICE   As good as done.

ISOBEL   Thank you. I wonder . . .

JANICE   Yes?

ISOBEL   What am I going to drink my coffee out of now?

JANICE exits. ISOBEL presses a button on her phone.

ISOBEL   Jenny?

JENNY   *(Voice)* Ma'am?

ISOBEL   Cancel all my meetings Friday afternoon.

JENNY   *(Voice)* But you've got—

ISOBEL   Just do it, please.

JENNY   Yes, ma'am.

Blackout.

SCENE SIX

We should be able to see ALEXANDRA and CHALMERS.
She in ISOBEL's living room. He in the meeting room.
She has her mobile phone, he uses a landline.

CHALMERS   You're ten minutes late.

ALEXANDRA   Sorry, I—

CHALMERS   It's not easy to do this, so you need to keep time.

ALEXANDRA   I'm sorry.

CHALMERS   If it's not fixed and clear, it doesn't work. Don't you understand where I am? It has to happen exactly like I say or it doesn't work – those are the rules!

ALEXANDRA   OK.

CHALMERS   *(Beat)* I'm sorry I shouted at you. Being in here can make you vulnerable to the worst parts of you.

ALEXANDRA   It's OK, it's my fault. Maybe we shouldn't even be doing this.

CHALMERS   But Alexandra, it's you who asked for *my* help.

ALEXANDRA   I know.

CHALMERS   And I have engaged honestly with you.

ALEXANDRA   I appreciate that.

CHALMERS   Thank you for not abandoning me when
            I told you who I really was.

ALEXANDRA   I know I'm really on the edge doing this. I
            mean, my mum … But this *is* where I want
            to be, talking about real things, revealing
            things, and I don't know if you can do that
            without risking breaking things.

CHALMERS   How much I hear your mother rise up in
            you at times.

ALEXANDRA   Do you hate me?

CHALMERS   No.

ALEXANDRA   You think that's what Mum did to you?

CHALMERS   Not absolutely. She didn't risk. Not like you.

ALEXANDRA   Just broke.

CHALMERS   We all break things. That drive you have,
            passion, youth and genes – you have the
            chance to define yourself.

ALEXANDRA   Crash – bang!

CHALMERS   Possibly. I completely understand why your
            mother did what she did. She thought she
            was right.

ALEXANDRA   But you think . . . I mean, you know she
              was wrong. You must hate her.

CHALMERS   I did hate her, blackly. But now I would like
              her to understand what she did.

ALEXANDRA   If we do this, she will.

CHALMERS   She might. And my family, Alexandra.

ALEXANDRA   I think I'm close to a structure for the
              documentary. I need your voice, though.

CHALMERS   That's tricky.

ALEXANDRA   I mean, there are these tapes with you
              speaking on that Mum's playing, but
              I don't think I can use them. Probably
              confidential.

CHALMERS   Probably.

JUDITH   *(Entering – to CHALMERS)* One minute.

ALEXANDRA   In the piece, I hear your voice and it's
              important.

CHALMERS   She's listening to the interview tapes?

ALEXANDRA   Has she been to see you?

CHALMERS   She's asked to talk to me. Has she got the
              case files with her?

ALEXANDRA   I don't know! It's just fucking typical.
              Amazingly, we meet, or make contact

through you following me on Twitter, I get
this great idea and there she is . . .

CHALMERS   Do you know what your mum is up to?

ALEXANDRA   Are you going to meet her? I know this can
work.

CHALMERS   Nobody ever knows if something will work.

JUDITH   Time, Alfred.

CHALMERS   Time's up: got to go. Goodbye.

ALEXANDRA   Bye . . . Bye.

She puts the phone down. Blackout.

SCENE SEVEN

FRANK revealed in ISOBEL's office. DREW enters.

FRANK   Where is she?

DREW   She's not here.

FRANK   Is that right?

DREW   Sorry.

FRANK   The future is in good hands with you now, isn't it? Do you know where she is?

DREW   She's taken the afternoon off.

FRANK   Right. Know why?

DREW   Getting a spray tan?

JANICE   *(Off)* Drew. We're moving. You need to be there now!

DREW hesitates.

FRANK   Well go then. Get the bad guys.

DREW   Sir.

He exits. FRANK paces, examines the desk. Nothing. Blackout.

SCENE EIGHT

A private room with a table, two chairs and security camera. JUDITH shows ISOBEL in. She is in civilian clothes.

JUDITH   I'll get him now. Take a seat.

ISOBEL   Thanks.

JUDITH goes. ISOBEL gets up and walks around the room. Her phone rings.

ISOBEL   *(Into phone)* Hello? *(Beat)* No, no, it's fine. *(Beat)* I know it's a peaceful protest, just keep them on George Street, it—

She hears a noise off.

ISOBEL   Can't talk, I'll call later.

She hangs up. ALFRED CHALMERS enters with JUDITH. He is in his sixties, grey, but the face has great definition. There is nothing amorphous about it. He sits down. No one speaks for a bit.

ISOBEL   Hello, Alfred. *(Beat)* You're looking well.
           (Beat) I appreciate you seeing me. And
           I'm sure you're wondering . . . why is she
           here? Why *am* I here? I suppose any kind
           of anniversary makes you think back to
           what was at the beginning, the thing that
           started it. And then you think of yourself
           and whether you've changed, not just
           older, but have the values changed, can
           you see things now that you couldn't then,
           appreciate things now that you couldn't
           then. And here we are again. Me. You.

CHALMERS   Still positively self-obsessed, I see: in that
           respect you have not changed.

ISOBEL   Aren't we all self-obsessed?

CHALMERS   I wasn't until I was put here, and then
           I found being self-obsessed preferable –
           (To JUDITH) no offence – to any kind of
           interest in those who surrounded me.

ISOBEL   I suppose so, it—

CHALMERS   You see, that's the worst of it – it's not the
           walls or the nurses; it's the fact that they
           hole you up with you. And twenty-five years
           is such a long time.

ISOBEL   It is.

CHALMERS   Oh you don't know the half of it.

ISOBEL	We've all had our journeys.
CHALMERS	Except I was denied mine.
ISOBEL	*(Beat)* Are you well?
CHALMERS	Do you mean physically?
ISOBEL	Yes.
CHALMERS	Yes. Because the court thought I must be mad, remember.
ISOBEL	I remember. Would you be prepared to talk to me?
CHALMERS	About?
ISOBEL	The whole thing?
CHALMERS	With you?
ISOBEL	With me.
CHALMERS	What's this?
ISOBEL	What do you mean?
CHALMERS	You got a wire?
ISOBEL	It's not American TV.
CHALMERS	Are you reopening my case?
ISOBEL	No. Not yet.
CHALMERS	Not yet?
ISOBEL	It depends.

CHALMERS   On what?

ISOBEL   Whether you give me a reason to.

CHALMERS   Is there new evidence?

ISOBEL   No.

CHALMERS   Well there never was any old evidence,
was there, Chief Constable – sorry,
Superintendent, Isobel McArthur. Didn't
get that job, did you? *(Beat)* I don't have
many visitors.

ISOBEL   No?

CHALMERS   Yes, funny, that.

ISOBEL   That must be difficult.

CHALMERS   Don't identify with me. You can't. I haven't
seen my wife or daughter in twenty-five
years. Not even a letter or a postcard.
I suppose I don't blame them, either of
them. I don't really hold them responsible.
How would you feel if your daughter
disappeared?

ISOBEL   How do you know I've got a daughter?

CHALMERS   Do you?

ISOBEL   *(Beat)* Yes.

CHALMERS   Right.

ISOBEL   You're here because I am interested in the
              truth. Are you interested in the truth?

CHALMERS   Depends on whose it is.

ISOBEL   Yours? I'm thinking of retiring.

CHALMERS   Thank God. Innocent people can once again
              sleep in peace at night.

ISOBEL   I thought I might write a book.

CHALMER   Why would that interest anybody?

ISOBEL   Maybe it won't.

CHALMERS   Except . . .

ISOBEL   Yes?

CHALMERS   Except if it had me in it.

ISOBEL   You are part of the journey.

CHALMERS   No, Isobel, I *am* your journey.

ISOBEL   You're part of it.

CHALMERS   What's on the tip of your tongue, Isobel?
              Something's desperate to get out but you
              won't let it.

ISOBEL   I am open to whatever you—

CHALMERS   Yes, yes, well that's a surprise, you open to
              me telling you things to sell your book.

ISOBEL   Does it matter, if it's about truth?

CHALMERS	Whose truth? You can't invent the truth.
ISOBEL	I don't want to invent the truth.
CHALMERS	But you sound like you've lost yours.
ISOBEL	No, I haven't.
CHALMERS	Now you want mine. And what for? What's in it for me?
ISOBEL	Tell the world.
CHALMERS	Tell the world what?
ISOBEL	Your story.
CHALMERS	Seeing you again. You're plain. Forgive me – hopefully you're past any vanity now. I can imagine you age of seven, waiting for Bobby Cefferty to choose you for the Gay Gordons. But he didn't. Went elsewhere. That other girl, remember her?
ISOBEL	Sadly, yes.
CHALMERS	Not sadly. That was the moment you realised that to be seen poor Isobel might need a lift to shine out.
ISOBEL	Is that how you started?
CHALMERS	Started? Is that the need? To be seen? To be seen to be right?
ISOBEL	I'm interested in justice. I don't care if I'm right.

CHALMERS   I have to say, bit insensitive not caring
            about being right, when I was sent down for
            you believing you were right.

ISOBEL   It wasn't just me, and there was evidence.

CHALMERS   My God, wobbly-kneed eighties forensics
            stumbling across the great divide of theory
            and hard-line evidence.

ISOBEL   You had her on you.

CHALMERS   Fibres. A few fibres. Not under fingernails
            but on my jacket. God, it sounded so
            scientific and sophisticated at the trial.

ISOBEL   You knew her.

CHALMERS   She was a patient where I worked as an
            orderly.

ISOBEL   It all added up.

CHALMERS   It isn't maths. It's not arithmetic in the
            classroom.

ISOBEL   Really?

CHALMERS   Is this it?

ISOBEL   Is this what?

CHALMERS   Just realised we might have started.

ISOBEL   Maybe we have.

CHALMERS   Don't fuck about with me. I'm not stupid.

ISOBEL   OK.

CHALMERS   Glib little answers. Don't you degrade me.

ISOBEL   I won't.

CHALMERS   Don't you degrade me any more than you
           already have done.

ISOBEL   I didn't degrade you.

CHALMERS   There's nothing you got I want.

ISOBEL   We talk, something is said, maybe it's good
           for you.

CHALMERS   Glib.

ISOBEL   I'm not promising anything, I'm not
           working for you here, but I *am* going to tell
           a story, and you're in it.

CHALMERS   It's my anniversary. But then you know
           that.

ISOBEL   And so someone might pay for this book.
           But maybe only now. Think.

CHALMERS   Can't have done much in the last twenty-
           five, eh? You want me to celebrate your old
           victory over me?

ISOBEL   It's not like that.

CHALMERS   I didn't do it.

(Beat)

ISOBEL   If we talk, then—

CHALMERS   Any of them.

ISOBEL   You say.

CHALMERS   I say.

ISOBEL   Then talk. Does a fox's head mean anything
            to you?

CHALMERS   A what?

ISOBEL   Someone in a . . . in a mask, fox, I think.

CHALMERS   No. Should it?

ISOBEL   I just get this picture of . . . it's stupid.

CHALMERS   I've thought about you a lot, and they are
            not nice thoughts.

ISOBEL   OK.

CHALMERS   Just being honest.

ISOBEL   I can take that.

CHALMER   Stop with the glib shit, or I walk.

ISOBEL   I'm sorry. I get it. I think about you too, and
            they are not nice thoughts.

CHALMERS   This meeting is about to end. You don't
            interest me, at least not face to face
            anyways.

ISOBEL   What does that mean?

CHALMERS   Ding dong, finished. *(To JUDITH)* Take me to my room, please.

ISOBEL   It's an opportunity.

CHALMERS   You had an opportunity and it was twenty-five years ago. But you took another road.

ISOBEL   I took the road I believed in.

CHALMERS   You're here to gloat and make money out of my lost years. All that life I could have had that you and your lot flattened!

He starts to leave.

ISOBEL   Isn't there anything you want said?

CHALMERS   Tell me if you have a doubt.

ISOBEL   What?

CHALMERS   Tell me if you have a doubt. About me.

ISOBEL   In what way?

CHALMERS   Going.

ISOBEL   There's lots of doubts around the case, we—

CHALMERS   Do you have a doubt or not?

ISOBEL   That you killed them?

CHALMERS   Yes, yes, that's right.

ISOBEL   I arrested you.

CHALMERS   Any doubt?

ISOBEL   I gave evidence at the trial. They were
            facts, it's not about—

CHALMERS   Is it there? Is there any doubt? Is there?
            Going, going, g—

ISOBEL   Yes.

CHALMERS   Thank you, Isobel. *(To JUDITH)* My room
            now, please. My room now.

CHALMERS exits, leaving ISOBEL alone.

SCENE NINE

ISOBEL arrives back at the same time as ALEXANDRA in a dressing gown or towel is taking the bag of files into the living room. It's a kind of collision that neither of them wants or was expecting.

ISOBEL   I thought you'd be at uni.

ALEXANDRA I thought you'd be at work. Were you?

ISOBEL   Yes.

ALEXANDRA Home early?

ISOBEL   Yes. That OK?

ALEXANDRA Why shouldn't it be?

ISOBEL   Well that's good then, isn't it? How's the project going?

ALEXANDRA Wow.

ISOBEL   What?

ALEXANDRA Never heard a question so uninterested in getting an answer.

ISOBEL   I do want to know.

ALEXANDRA Let's not do this.

ISOBEL	What's that, love?
ALEXANDRA	Are you here? When you're here, are you here? The talk that isn't a talk. I'm fluent in talking to you in your absence.
ISOBEL	What does that mean?
ALEXANDRA	It means I am so mixed up about when you were actually here when I was young but not here. And then sometimes not here at all.
ISOBEL	What are you talking about: is this postmodernist talk?
ALEXANDRA	I don't know what it is, Mum.
ISOBEL	I'm trying to do something that is important to me.
ALEXANDRA	So am I.
ISOBEL	I know. I'd love to see what you've got so far.
ALEXANDRA	Not yet. God, even now, when you've achieved everything, you're still grabbing for it.
ISOBEL	Grabbing for what?
ALEXANDRA	The centre.
ISOBEL	It's not about that.

ALEXANDRA Well you tell me what it is you're trying to solve, Chief Superintendent Isobel. What's it about?

ISOBEL It's about trying to understand what I've been doing for thirty years.

ALEXANDRA That sounds like a big fat me.

ISOBEL It's a book. Money. Maybe a wee bit of salvation.

ALEXANDRA Do you need that? Salvation?

ISOBEL Maybe that's why I'm writing the book. How could you say that!

ALEXANDRA Say what, Mum?

ISOBEL About me being the centre of things.

ALEXANDRA I only meant you being the centre of you. You see, you had to have actually been there to be at the centre of my world.

ISOBEL Oh I was there, Alexandra.

ALEXANDRA I can't fix you in my past sometimes. I sometimes see us sitting at the dinner table but then you're not there. Where were you? Was it actually me alone at the dinner table?

ISOBEL I was there. It's the stress—

ALEXANDRA   But then I have a keen memory of you with
             a three-tiered jelly, all circus colours.

ISOBEL   You see – you might even have had fun in
             your childhood.

*The sound of music suddenly kicks up in the room off. We
can hear a man whooping, mock-rapping along. ISOBEL
and ALEXANDRA look at each other for a while.*

ISOBEL   So that's why you're not at uni.

ALEXANDRA   You're going to write about *him*. He's your
             star, isn't he?

ISOBEL   He's a part of it.

ALEXANDRA   Big part?

ISOBEL   At the moment, he's a significant part, yes.

ALEXANDRA   A monster?

ISOBEL   Could be.

ALEXANDRA   Don't you know? Well if he's not, then who's
             the monster?

*A knocking at the door. ALEXANDRA mouths along
to the music off and slowly withdraws to the bedroom.
ISOBEL looks about her, seeing the files. She grabs
some and puts them in a pile somewhere, leaving
the others to lie. She answers the door. It is Frank.
He is drunk and staggers inside.*

FRANK   I know it's early, but I had the afternoon off, and there's the Alhambra in Leith where irresponsible men go: so I went and it was uncomfortable – for them, owing to me having done them over a range of misdemeanours – but I did get served, and kept getting served and then it went a bit blurry.

ISOBEL   Do come in, Frank.

FRANK   *(Puzzled)* I *am* in. Been a while. Suddenly remembered. Fuck. This place. You live here. You fucking—

ISOBEL   Not into this, Frank.

FRANK   I know, but—

ISOBEL   And you said you'd never bring it up, so if you are so drunk that you can't keep your word, then get out.

FRANK   Sorry. I'm done now. Two people. You and me. Alone.

ISOBEL   I'm not alone.

FRANK   Yes, I know you've got Alex, but you know. How is Alex, by the way?

ISOBEL   She lacks any drive other than a sex drive.

FRANK   So normal, then?

ISOBEL   No, Frank, I don't think so.

FRANK   You can't remember? See, I did try. I got married. But I don't know that I should have. How many years was I miserable? How long was she miserable, poor cow? Poor cow who takes my money with a little flat on North Berwick High Street and manages to keep busy by book clubs and the Shipwrecked Fishermen and Mariners' Royal Benevolent Society. Do fishermen still get shipwrecked?

ISOBEL   Yes.

FRANK   And even though it is an absolutely brilliant fact that she is gone, her leaving has not led to . . . to the next thing.

ISOBEL   Go home, Frank.

FRANK   What's at home?

ISOBEL   Sky Sports.

FRANK   Oh, you're good.

ISOBEL   I know.

FRANK   Men go into their caves. Shamed by our thinning hair, springless knees and whatnot. My penis still works, though – it's still tip-top.

ISOBEL   That's just wonderful for you, Frank.

FRANK   Thanks, Isobel. I'll pass it on.

ISOBEL   By all means.

FRANK   Unless you'd like to say it personally.

ISOBEL   No, I trust you with the message.

FRANK   If you're sure.

ISOBEL   I'm sure.

FRANK   Right.

ISOBEL   My oh my. That felt a little close to the edge,
         Frank. Where did that come from?

FRANK   *(Examining the windows)* Should put locks on
         this.

ISOBEL   This is Merchiston, Frank.

FRANK   We could do it here.

ISOBEL   What?

FRANK   On the couch. Now.

ISOBEL   No.

*FRANK makes a move on her. It's not rough but drunkenly
direct.*

FRANK   Come on.

ISOBEL   No!

FRANK tries again.

FRANK   Come on. It's a good thing. It's a good thing.

ISOBEL   Get off! Stop it. Where did that come from? We haven't for, for—

FRANK   Nearly twenty-five years. You know, maybe it just brings it all back, Isobel. Maybe I thought, well, if the bad shit like him is on its way back up, then maybe some of the good things from then could be too. Because it was good, Isobel.

ISOBEL   Not so good that it lasted.

FRANK   So you can revisit *that*. *(Indicates files or cassettes)* But you can't *this*.

ISOBEL   That's right. There is nothing unresolved about us, Frank.

FRANK   Well maybe it's not about something being unresolved; maybe it's how I feel now, on this day, at this time.

ISOBEL   So you come round here for what? For a shag and a—

FRANK   Because I needed comfort and I thought you might be the only one to give it to me.

ISOBEL   You'd have screwed me and what?

FRANK   Tea and toast?

ISOBEL   Can't believe you're saying this. Go home and have a wank, Frank, you'll feel better.

FRANK   Can't you remember what it was like?

ISOBEL   Frank, it's . . . We are friends.

FRANK   Friends?

ISOBEL   *(Firm)* Friends, yes.

FRANK   Right. *(Beat)* I called at the office today.

ISOBEL   I wasn't there.

FRANK   You weren't there.

ISOBEL   Ah-ha.

FRANK   OK.

ISOBEL   OK.

FRANK   I like your young copper, what's her name?

ISOBEL   Janice.

FRANK   Janice, that's it.

ISOBEL   Bit young for—

FRANK   I'm not a hound dog, Isobel.

ISOBEL   That reference is your father's generation.

FRANK   He's still the King.

ISOBEL   His fat death happened nearly forty years ago.

FRANK   Don't take it out on Elvis, Isobel.

ISOBEL   I'm sorry, Frank.

The sound of sex in the next room.

FRANK   That's a bit . . .

ISOBEL   Yes.

FRANK   How do you . . . ?

ISOBEL   Well, you just do.

FRANK   It's your house.

ISOBEL   It's our house. It's pretty relentless. Frank, I
         saw Chalmers. I know you'd want to know and
         I think it's reasonable that I tell you. I met
         him.

FRANK   Right.

ISOBEL   Right?

FRANK   Well, what can I say?

ISOBEL   What you think.

FRANK   I've told you that. You still did it.

ISOBEL   I think he wants to tell the truth.

FRANK   Does he?

ISOBEL   I think so.

FRANK   And you'd trust Chalmers with something so
         precious as the truth?

ISOBEL   I need the truth.

FRANK   You had . . . you *have* the truth.

ISOBEL   I don't know.

FRANK   You do know.

ISOBEL   What wrong can come of this, Frank? I mean,
           it's talk.

FRANK   What wrong can come of it? Hasn't it already
           started?

ISOBEL   What . . . ?

FRANK   I got to call you on this, Isobel, and beg, and
           not for entirely altruistic reasons, that you
           stop this.

ISOBEL   I hear you. No.

FRANK   Right.

ISOBEL   You could help me.

FRANK   You're joking.

ISOBEL   I don't understand why—

FRANK   Because he's a nightmare, Isobel. The *idea*
           of him stinks up the place and people start
           choking. He sends a sliver of metal screaming
           through your nervous system. He's like some
           kind of fucked-up high. I like golf and I like
           getting the people who are about to do crime
           before they get a chance. And if I can't, then
           I'll get them after. That's my sworn duty. And
           that's my life. It might be small and not very
           wide, but it gets me up in the morning, maybe
           not always with a smile on my face, but I

know why my life is moving forward and as a consequence I can pay my maintenance and my Sky Sports package.

ALEXANDRA has appeared at the doorway.

ALEXANDRA   Thought I heard voices. Hello, Uncle Frank.

FRANK   Hello . . . God, you've grown up.

ALEXANDRA   You saw me six months ago. Just thought I'd check by in case Mum had brought back any strange men.

FRANK   Only me . . .

ALEXANDRA   Have you offered Uncle Frank a drink yet, Mum?

ISOBEL   I think Frank's had enough.

FRANK   Depends.

ALEXANDRA   Look at all the homework Mum has, Uncle Frank, she's got even more than me.

ISOBEL   What's got into you?

ALEXANDRA   Well . . .

ISOBEL   I've got to get some air.

ALEXANDRA   There's some outside.

ISOBEL   Thanks.

ALEXANDRA   Not much inside.

ISOBEL starts to exit.

ALEXANDRA We'll get a pizza later, or have you—

ISOBEL Sorry.

ALEXANDRA No, it's OK.

ISOBEL No, it's not, I should—

ALEXANDRA Ah, should.

ISOBEL Yes.

ALEXANDRA *(Playful)* Old should've.

ISOBEL Going.

ALEXANDRA OK.

FRANK Go, it's fine. Listen, don't forget Fergus. He's still in there.

ISOBEL Shit.

FRANK Yeah.

ALEXANDRA Happy walking.

ISOBEL Love you.

ISOBEL exits.

ALEXANDRA You too. Is she allowed to bring all that home with her? Is this strictly legal, Frank?

FRANK Strictly?

ALEXANDRA Yes, strictly, by letter of law.

FRANK No.

ALEXANDRA Then why not arrest her?

FRANK Because this is all . . . It's all done, it's
nothing.

ALEXANDRA Then why has Chief Superintendent
McArthur filled her house with all this
nothing?

FRANK It'll pass.

ALEXANDRA You sure?

FRANK She's just trying to sort things out.

ALEXANDRA Well, good to know she's keeping busy.

FRANK You show your mum a little respect now,
Alex.

ALEXANDRA What was that?

FRANK She deserves your respect. Your mum is
. . . is substantial.

ALEXANDRA She's not that fat.

FRANK You know, Alex, don't be so light with things
– you can lose them that way.

ALEXANDRA Ooooh. Deep. Deep deep. Reminds me –
better go. Lovely seeing you, Uncle Frank.

FRANK   Don't try and be so clever, Alexandra.
               Stay innocent as long as you can.

ALEXANDRA   She's visiting Alfred Chalmers, isn't she?

FRANK   Yes.

ALEXANDRA   Do you think it's a good thing?

FRANK   No, I don't.

ALEXANDRA   Not good to check the past for truth and
               lies?

FRANK   That's a dark road. Your mum loves you.
               She's only ever done what she thinks was
               best for you. That's all you need to know.

ALEXANDRA   I don't know, Uncle Frank, I don't know
               how much I really believe that. I think she
               did what was best for her. I think that's
               what she always does. That's what I think
               even if I don't want to think it.

FRANK   That's a shame.

YOUNG MAN   *(Off)* Come on, Alexandra!

FRANK   It'll be OK. Nothing bad is going to happen.

ALEXANDRA   You make it sound like something might.

FRANK   No.

YOUNG MAN   *(Off)* Alexandra!

ALEXANDRA   Coming! Uncle Frank?

FRANK   Yes?

ALEXANDRA   I'd like you to fuck off now.

FRANK   Sure, Alex.

FRANK goes to leave.

YOUNG MAN   *(Off)* Come on!

FRANK   If you need anything, you know, just—

ALEXANDRA   I know. Thanks.

FRANK exits. ALEXANDRA picks up a file, looks at it.

YOUNG MAN   *(Off)* Alexandra. Alexandra, I'm lonely.
             I'm soooo lonely.

ALEXANDRA   Coming.

ALEXANDRA exits.

Act Two

SCENE ONE

ALEXANDRA alone. House. Quiet. CHALMERS on the phone.

CHALMERS   On time.

ALEXANDRA   Hello.

CHALMERS   *(Pause)* Are you still there?

ALEXANDRA   Yes.

CHALMERS   Don't you want to talk?

ALEXANDRA   I don't know.

CHALMERS   Has something upset you?

ALEXANDRA   I want to commit.

CHALMERS   Good.

ALEXANDRA   I mean to this. I'll do everything to make it happen.

CHALMERS   That's good.

ALEXANDRA   That is, if you still want to. *(Beat)* Do you?

CHALMERS   I have to think of my situation, Alexandra.

ALEXANDRA   I knew it, she's going to fuck this up for me. She's completely self-obsessed.

CHALMERS   If she is rethinking or even looking at my case then that could be significant in making things happen for me.

ALEXANDRA   I thought that's what *we* were doing.

CHALMERS   Of course, but Alexandra, your mother is the chief superintendent of Edinburgh police, and the person who arrested me.

ALEXANDRA   And I'm a flaky student making a documentary. If we get this right, it could open everything right up. I won't let you down. You're not going to dump me, are you?

CHALMERS   No.

ALEXANDRA   She wins again. OK, let's drop it.

CHALMERS   Wait! How would it be if I send you some spoken words?

ALEXANDRA   How?

CHALMERS   The post.

ALEXANDRA   Can you do that?

CHALMERS   I'm sure I can find a way.

ALEXANDRA OK.

CHALMERS I'll put some thoughts down about . . . then.
Would that help move things on?

ALEXANDRA Yes. Yes, it would.

CHALMERS OK.

ALEXANDRA Do you want my address?

CHALMERS Would be useful.

Pause as ALEXANDRA hesitates.

CHALMERS Or we could forget it.

ALEXANDRA No, no I—

CHALMERS I'm not interested in not being trusted. You
say you want me to trust you, but you're
not sure about giving me your address?

ALEXANDRA It's 121 Polwarth Gardens EH11 1LQ. *(Beat.
A little panicked)* Hello, are you still there,
Alfred?

CHALMERS Is this a joke?

ALEXANDRA No. What's wrong?

CHALMERS Are you playing with me?

ALEXANDRA No, what's wrong?

CHALMERS That's interesting. Now that's a subject for
a book, Alexandra.

ALEXANDRA   What do you mean?

CHALMERS   I liked your last blog on the film festival.

ALEXANDRA   It's just words. Our piece will use visuals.
              What did you mean about my address?

CHALMERS   Nothing. Any pieces of paper hanging about
              with her thoughts written on them? You
              could look now.

ALEXANDRA   But—

CHALMERS   It's important to me.

ALEXANDRA   *(Moves to the files and picks them up)* Just the
              case files. She circled a couple of things;
              well, it looks fresh.

CHALMERS   Yes?

ALEXANDRA   'Sample fibre from victim's clothing found
              on suspect.' She's written 'Find' next to it.
              She's got all … all the four victims, with
              a column for each and lots of stuff about
              them. There's a dark line between Sarah
              McElhenney and the other ones.

CHALMERS   That's very useful, Alexandra, thank you.
              Let's keep talking.

ALEXANDRA   Oh, do you have to go? I was just going to
              give you my first storyboard ideas – though
              what you send me might change that, so—

CHALMERS   Let's talk when you get what I send you.

ALEXANDRA What? Oh, right. Exciting.

CHALMERS Yes, it's exciting. It's on the move.

ALEXANDRA What is? Right. Right.

CHALMERS hangs up. Blackout.

SCENE TWO

ISOBEL revealed, sitting at her desk. It's hard to tell whether she is sleeping or thinking. JANICE enters, stands unsure as to whether to enter properly. Finally . . .

JANICE   Ma'am? Ma'am?

ISOBEL   Yes?

JANICE   Are you all right?

ISOBEL   What is it, Janice?

JANICE   Inspector Ryan wants to know if he can talk about the Prince Harry visit.

ISOBEL   Does he? Yes, but not with me.

JANICE   *(Beat)* Right, I'll tell him then.

ISOBEL   A minute, Janice. Have you been on to Records about the forensics sample from the Chalmers case?

JANICE   They're looking, I think.

ISOBEL   'I think' offers nothing to me. How hard is it to find? Check again.

JANICE   Will do, ma'am. Do you want a coffee?

ISOBEL   I would kill for a coffee.

JANICE   That might put me in a difficult position.

ISOBEL laughs, then JANICE. FRANK knocks and enters.

FRANK   Morning.

ISOBEL   Janice was just about to make coffee.

FRANK   Funny, when I ask someone in my department
           for a coffee, all I get is a resentful look and no
           sugar. Problem with the young. When I started,
           I saw all demeaning and abusive behaviour as
           a valuable part of my training.

JANICE   Would you like a coffee too, sir?

FRANK   Do you know, I would. Four sugars.

JANICE   Four?

FRANK   Hot and sweet.

JANICE exits. Beat.

ISOBEL   What did you want?

FRANK   Just checking in. How are things?

ISOBEL   Fine.

FRANK   Good.

ISOBEL   Lied.

FRANK   I know. She's angry.

ISOBEL   Maybe that's OK and I have to live with that.

FRANK   Sure. *(Beat)* Sorry I was a bit drunk.

ISOBEL   It's OK.

FRANK   No, you've got enough to be getting on with without me being all loved-up nostalgic.

ISOBEL   It's fine, I'm a big girl.

FRANK   But you must know that if you keep digging around then you are definitely going to throw up some nasty shit.

ISOBEL   Yes, thanks for the metaphor, Frank.

FRANK   It's going to get worse. You OK with that?

ISOBEL   Yes.

FRANK   Right.

ISOBEL   Right.

FRANK   It's not there. I looked.

ISOBEL   What isn't?

FRANK   The fibre.

ISOBEL   You found the box.

FRANK   My world for many years.

ISOBEL   Where was it?

FRANK   It was there.

ISOBEL   No it wasn't. I've been asking them for days.
         They told me—

FRANK   Should have asked me.

ISOBEL   You didn't seem inclined.

FRANK   I'm a friend.

ISOBEL   How could it not be there?

FRANK   I don't know.

ISOBEL   That's a pretty important piece of evidence,
         Frank.

FRANK   From a case twenty-five years old for which
         there have been no appeals in twenty-four.
         It couldn't be more dead.

ISOBEL   Was everything else there?

FRANK   Dunno. Think so.

ISOBEL   So what happened to it?

FRANK   I don't know.

ISOBEL   Fucking hell, Frank, does that not seem
         suspicious to you?

FRANK   No.

ISOBEL   No?

FRANK   It happens.

ISOBEL   Does it – how?

FRANK   It was a few strands in a plastic fucking bag
          – a rogue gust of wind sneaking through a
          corridor could have magicked it away.

ISOBEL   Not buying it.

FRANK   Well maybe you're just too keen to see what
          you want to see.

ISOBEL   That's what he said about us. That fibre put
          him away.

FRANK   No, killing those girls did that.

ISOBEL   And the fibre on him that seemed to match up
          with Sarah McElhenney's coat.

FRANK   Not *seemed* to, Isobel – *did*!

ISOBEL   Can I have it?

FRANK   Have what?

ISOBEL   The box.

FRANK   There's not much in it, just—

ISOBEL   Can I have it?

FRANK   Yes, you can have it.

ISOBEL   When?

FRANK   Whenever you want.

ISOBEL   Can you get hold of Sarah's box too: her
          things?

FRANK   What for?

ISOBEL   I want to see them, Frank. Can you do that?

FRANK   Yes.

ISOBEL   I'm free tomorrow night. Can you bring it to
         me then?

FRANK   Off duty? So it's not a police matter, then?

ISOBEL   Not yet.

FRANK   It's not official?

ISOBEL   Not yet.

FRANK   Filled in the forms?

ISOBEL   No.

FRANK   No form?

ISOBEL   Don't play with me, Frank. *(Beat)* Don't even
         think of saying that thought out loud. Can you
         bring them?

FRANK   OK. The Central bar. Eight o'clock.

ISOBEL   An unsavoury place.

FRANK   Perfect, then, I suppose. Isobel, the mistake
         can easily be made where the fear of your
         future slips doubts into what's been, about
         how you got to now. You need to concentrate on
         what's next for you. The past is an immovable
         object; it's dark and heavy, and the longer you
         look into the darkness, the more your eyes
         seem to see things that aren't there.

ISOBEL My goodness, Frank, that was pretty poetic for a boy from Cardiff's mean streets.

FRANK You're like a sister.

ISOBEL Thank you, that's nice.

FRANK A sister I'd give one to.

ISOBEL That's not so nice, Frank.

FRANK It could be.

ISOBEL What was it you were saying about the past? *(Beat)* Frank, I keep getting a picture of, I don't know why, a fox's head. Does that mean anything to you?

FRANK No.

ISOBEL OK.

JANICE and DREW enter.

JANICE Coffee.

FRANK *(Indicates ISOBEL)* Chief Superintendent McArthur could do with both. I'll get on with the nasty stuff on the streets.

ISOBEL I'll have to take this with me.

ISOBEL exits.

FRANK Do you think he's attractive?

JANICE   Sir?

FRANK   Prince Harry. How can anyone . . . ?

JANICE   He's mythical. He's a prince. We need that bit
          of glamour.

FRANK   No we don't.

JANICE exits. DREW lingers.

DREW   How do I get your job?

FRANK   You can't, it's mine.

DREW   I mean, when you're—

FRANK   Dead? Well, you need a bit of that: bit of cold,
          bit of ruthless. You got that?

DREW   I think so.

FRANK   Well, when you know it, let me know and
          we'll talk.

DREW   I have.

FRANK   OK. Thomson's at six. You buy the drinks.

DREW   Anything.

ISOBEL enters.

ISOBEL   What you two up to?

FRANK   Career guidance.

ISOBEL   Drew, you look suspicious.

DREW   No, ma'am.

FRANK   Well, I'm off.

ISOBEL   Remember the briefing on staffing Thursday.
You need to get your projections ready or you'll
lose the argument.

FRANK   I am great at arguing.

ISOBEL   Not what I'm saying.

FRANK   Till tomorrow.

FRANK exits with DREW.

ISOBEL   *(Calls off)* Janice.

JANICE enters.

JANICE   Ma'am?

ISOBEL   When you asked them about the Chalmers
evidence box, what did they say?

JANICE   Just that they were finding it hard to locate it.

ISOBEL   So it wasn't where it should have been?

JANICE   I don't think it's as straightforward as that. I
was down in Records for a few weeks, and you
know the scene in *Raiders of the Lost Ark* at the
end when you see the warehouse full of crates?

ISOBEL   Really.

JANICE   Various times people have obviously decided
          to improve the filing system, so, depending
          on which year, it depends on which system
          and then it depends on whether someone
          went back and tried to apply the new system
          retrospectively. Or not. If you see what I mean.

ISOBEL   Kind of. Go ask Inspector Ryan to come and
          see me.

JANICE   Any particular reason shall I tell him?

ISOBEL   The trouble with Harry.

JANICE   I think he's sweet.

ISOBEL   Indeed.

JANICE   Ma'am.

  JANICE exits.

SCENE THREE

ALEXANDRA enters her home, carrying a camera. She picks up her post. She opens a small package and takes out a USB stick. She sticks it in the computer, pours herself a drink. Whilst she is doing so, the USB has gone to autoplay.

CHALMERS   *(Voice from computer)* Good evening, Alexandra. Listen to the cassettes. Listen to the interview on November the fifth, 1988. Yes, that's Bonfire Night.

MUSIC suddenly plays from the computer. It's 'Teddy Bear's Picnic'.

ALEXANDRA   What the . . . ? Is that all? Come on. Come on.

She goes to the cassettes, rummages till she finds one, puts it on.

CHALMERS   *(Voice from cassette)* You're corrupted, Isobel. I see you in the middle of the road. I can see you and you don't know what to do, what to decide.

ISOBEL   *(Voice from cassette)* I'm always very careful crossing the road. I need to ask you where you were on September the seventeenth, 1988 from seven p.m.—

CHALMERS   *(Voice from cassette)* How much do you trust your colleagues?

FERGUS   *(Voice from cassette)* Where's this going, Alfred?

FRANK   *(Voice from cassette)* You not done the decent thing yet, Chalmers?

CHALMERS   *(Voice from cassette)* If I did, would you be capable of recognising it?

FRANK   *(Voice from cassette)* Clever.

CHALMERS   *(Voice from cassette)* No, that's not clever, at least not to an intelligent man.

ISOBEL   *(Voice from cassette)* Detective Inspector Frank Bowman has entered the room at eleven thirty-four a.m.

FERGUS   *(Voice from cassette)* So tell me about Sarah McElhenney, from 121 Polwarth Gardens.

CHALMERS   *(Voice from cassette)* I've never been there.

FERGUS   *(Voice from cassette)* But you know that's her address?

CHALMERS   *(Voice from cassette)* I don't know anything about her.

ALEXANDRA stops and rewinds the tape.

FERGUS   *(Voice from cassette)* ... Sarah McElhenney, from 121 Polwarth Gardens.

CHALMERS   I've never—

She does it again.

FERGUS   *(Voice from cassette)* ... from 121 Polwarth Gardens.

Stops. Rewinds it again.

FERGUS   *(Voice from cassette)* ... McElhenney, from 121 Polwarth Gardens.

Stops tape. Gets up, moves around.

ALEXANDRA   Fuck. *(Beat)* Fuck fuck fuck. No no no no no. Come on. Fuck. No way. Fuck. Joking. How ... ? Oh no. No.

Laughing off. ISOBEL and FRANK enter. They've had a drink. ISOBEL carries the evidence box.

ISOBEL   I'm afraid your mum has dropped the baton of good and proper behaviour ...

FRANK   It was me! I tripped her up.

ISOBEL   ... but I kind of think it's healthy, y'know, to surprise your children—

ALEXANDRA   Were you never going to tell me?

ISOBEL   About what?

FRANK   You being an alcoholic.

ISOBEL   I'm not an alchol . . . alcoholic.

FRANK   That sounded so bad.

ALEXANDRA   About our house.

ISOBEL   What about our house?

ALEXANDRA walks over to cassette player, rewinds.

ISOBEL   You shouldn't be playing those, Alexandra,
             it's—

CHALMERS   *(Voice from cassette)* . . . not clever, at least
             not to an intelligent man.

FERGUS   *(Voice from cassette)* So tell me about Sarah
             McElhenney, from 121 Polwarth Gardens.

CHALMERS   *(Voice from cassette)* I've never been there.

FERGUS   *(Voice from cassette)* And her?

ALEXANDRA stops the cassette.

ALEXANDRA   That's our address.

ISOBEL   Yes.

ALEXANDRA   That's our home.

ISOBEL   Yes.

ALEXANDRA Mum?

ISOBEL   I know.

ALEXANDRA And?

ISOBEL   Please can we talk about this in the
           morning, when I'm—

ALEXANDRA No! No, we can't do that. We're living in
           Sarah McElhenney's house?

ISOBEL   No, it's our house.

ALEXANDRA You know what I mean!

ISOBEL   Yes, yes, I do. I'm sorry.

ALEXANDRA What for?

ISOBEL   Everything you're feeling right now.

ALEXANDRA You have no idea what I'm feeling right
           now.

ISOBEL   No, I suppose not.

FRANK   Alexandra, you also don't know what it felt
           like back then, not just the investigation,
           the trial, but afterwards, it was—

ALEXANDRA What was it? How fucked up is that? You
           bought one of the victims' houses. Why?

FRANK backs off.

ISOBEL   I don't know.

ALEXANDRA   Why did you do it?

ISOBEL   I don't know.

ALEXANDRA   Of course you know. How could you not
              know?

ISOBEL   I can't.

ALEXANDRA   Can't what?

ISOBEL   Sorry?

ALEXANDRA   What? What is this? No, Mother, you owe
              me answers here. I've grown up in a . . .
              Wait: where?

ISOBEL   What?

ALEXANDRA   Where?

ISOBEL   Darling.

ALEXANDRA   Don't do that.

ISOBEL   Sorry. Things have been stressful. I know.

ALEXANDRA   No you don't.

ISOBEL   And I want you to know that . . .

ALEXANDRA   Oh God, where?

ISOBEL   . . . I never did anything that I believed
              could ever harm you.

ALEXANDRA   Well you were wrong, Mum, you're—

ISOBEL   I know, I see that – sorry.

ALEXANDRA   Stop saying that stupid useless word.
Where was she found?

ISOBEL   Oh, Alexandra.

ALEXANDRA   Just tell me. Where?

ISOBEL   I . . .

ALEXANDRA   Oh God, not . . .

ISOBEL   What?

ALEXANDRA   Not in . . . not in my . . .

ISOBEL   No, no, not there.

ALEXANDRA   Right.

ISOBEL   Right. No, no.

ALEXANDRA   Where?

ISOBEL   It was – it was under the floorboards.
That's where we found her.

ALEXANDRA   Which ones?

ISOBEL   Which ones? Just Sarah.

ALEXANDRA   *Which ones?*

ISOBEL   Oh – I thought you meant which . . . You
mean the room.

ALEXANDRA   Yes.

ISOBEL   That's good because . . . It was there.

(Beat)

ALEXANDRA OK.

ISOBEL   I never imagined you would ever know.

ALEXANDRA What treacheries riddle history with that
             motif.

ISOBEL   *(A little biting)* That from one of your
             projects?

ALEXANDRA Why, Mum? Why? A dead girl.

ISOBEL   The house was cheap. Her parents needed
             to sell! You weren't even born. It was years
             before . . . *(Beat)* I needed to be close to her,
             maybe. I wasn't coping. I didn't tell anyone
             till after I'd bought . . . I can't explain.

ALEXANDRA Have you any other secrets? Where does my
             memory of things stop being real?

ISOBEL   You know your own life.

ALEXANDRA No I don't. I don't.

ISOBEL   For God's sake.

ALEXANDRA Who is my father?

ISOBEL   Don't ask that! We agreed to never—

ALEXANDRA And I'm not agreeing any more. Who is he?

ISOBEL	I told you, I—
ALEXANDRA	Is he under the floorboards too? *(Beat)* Oh my God . . .
ISOBEL	Of course he's not under the floorboards!
ALEXANDRA	Is he under the floorboards, Isobel?
ISOBEL	He's not under the floorboards.
ALEXANDRA	Is my dad . . . What am I saying? OK. I can't stay here now.
ISOBEL	It was a long time ago.
ALEXANDRA	No. It was today.
ISOBEL	Please.
ALEXANDRA	I can't.
ISOBEL	Oh Alex.
ALEXANDRA	No, I can't. I have to go.
ISOBEL	Don't – you're everything.
ALEXANDRA	No I'm not. And I never have been. So stop lying.
ISOBEL	I'm sorry.
ALEXANDRA	I'm going.
FRANK	Don't let him do this.
ALEXANDRA	Who?

FRANK   Chalmers – he caused this.

ALEXANDRA   No he didn't.

ISOBEL   You didn't need to know.

ALEXANDRA   Should have kept the lie up?

ISOBEL   There were no lies – I just didn't say.
             For you.

ALEXANDRA   It's ghoulish.

FRANK   When you're dealing with monsters . . .

ALEXANDRA   She's not sure he is a monster. *(To ISOBEL)*
             You know you're not. *(Beat)* So I can also
             tell you now that the project I'm working on
             is with him.

ISOBEL   Who?

ALEXANDRA   Alfred.

FRANK   Alfred? *Alfred?* You're fucking joking.

ALEXANDRA   We made contact months ago, long before
             you came up with your book idea. I saw the
             silver jubilee coming before *you* did! I'm
             going to do a documentary about him.

ISOBEL   You can't.

ALEXANDRA   You can't say that any more.

FRANK   Have you talked with him?

ALEXANDRA   On the phone.

FRANK What do you think you're doing?

ALEXANDRA I think I'm getting on with my life.

ISOBEL This is to get at me, isn't it?

ALEXANDRA No, this is to get at *me*! Because it seems to me my past isn't what I thought it was at all. Because all the time you were Mum to me and with me, you had *her* in our home, in *you* too. You had a ghost with you and she was part of us and that means, must mean, that we are not what I thought we actually were.

ISOBEL It's not true.

ALEXANDRA You don't know what's true. And neither do I.

FRANK Please stay away from him.

ALEXANDRA *She* couldn't.

ISOBEL That's different. I was involved.

ALEXANDRA And now *I* am. And that's because of you, Mum, don't forget. I'm going to pack now.

ISOBEL Don't go.

ALEXANDRA Have to. I can't stay here.

ALEXANDRA exits to her room.

ISOBEL What do I do?

FRANK   Let her go.

ISOBEL   Just let her go?

FRANK   For now.

ISOBEL   For how long? That's easy for you . . . She can't
          leave.

FRANK   You don't have a choice.

ISOBEL   Of course I do.

FRANK   You're not chief here.

ISOBEL   Oh Frank, what have I done?

FRANK   Well we did all wonder that at the time, when
          you eventually told us, I mean. We knew you
          were struggling.

ISOBEL   You took care of me, you and Fergus. Why did
          I do that? I think I had forgotten. Had I?
          It's a pretty fucked-up thing to do.

FRANK   It *was* a pretty fucked-up thing to do.

ISOBEL   How do I explain that to my daughter?

FRANK   You can't, I think.

ISOBEL   Then what do I do?

FRANK   You have to accept you're not in control.

ALEXANDRA enters with a bag.

ALEXANDRA   I'm going to Lilly's.

FRANK   I'll get you a cab.

ISOBEL   I could—

ALEXANDRA   I don't want anything from you.

ISOBEL   I'll get you some money, some cash in case you . . .

ISOBEL exits.

FRANK   Don't let him work on you, Alexandra.
He'll make it confused, then offer you
clarity. Keep away from him. Please.

ALEXANDRA   Why?

FRANK   Why?

ALEXANDRA   Yes, why?

FRANK   He hurts people.

ALEXANDRA   Maybe.

FRANK   Maybe?

ALEXANDRA   Maybe.

FRANK   Your mother helped condemn him. If you
were him, how would you feel about you?

ALEXANDRA   What a mind-bending question.

FRANK   What's on your mind?

ALEXANDRA   What do you mean?

FRANK   Doesn't help: you putting it about.
The noise.

ALEXANDRA   That's got nothing to do with you. No more
about that, Frank.

FRANK   What's it about?

ALEXANDRA   Sex.

FRANK   Really?

ALEXANDRA   Women now enjoy sex; it's not like when
you were young.

FRANK   Your eyes.

ALEXANDRA   You making a move on me now?

FRANK   They're like those pictures of houses or
villages after a flood.

ALEXANDRA   That's very poetic of you. Mum's been ages.
Do you think she's having a shit? *(Beat)*
So you knew.

FRANK   Of course I knew.

ALEXANDRA   Didn't think to say anything? *(Beat)* Know
what's weird? I think maybe there's nothing
weird about this at all. That's what's weird.

FRANK   Maybe.

ALEXANDRA   Yes, maybe. Are you my father, Frank?

FRANK   What?

ALEXANDRA   Yes or no.

FRANK   Alex, you—

ALEXANDRA   You see, there's this tide of revelation and review in the air and I'm kind of bobbing along with its pull, and so it would be good to know about any, you know, tidal surges or whirlpools I didn't know about.

FRANK   You asked your mum about this?

ALEXANDRA   Because, amazingly, I'm nearly twenty-two and I still don't know who my—

FRANK   I know, I—

ALEXANDRA   Are you my fucking father, Frank?

FRANK   No. No, I'm not.

ALEXANDRA   OK, because I'm just trying to get some clarity here and I suppose knowing some things aren't true is some kind of start.

FRANK   I get it.

ALEXANDRA   I don't! I don't get any of this! I'm in a fucking dead person's house. What do you think of that?

FRANK   It's unusual.

ALEXANDRA   Frank. That's . . . that's just very true.

FRANK   If you were my daughter I'd be proud, and
            I have always tried to be there, you know,
            if you, if you . . .

ALEXANDRA   I know, Uncle Frank.

FRANK   I don't know who your father is, Alexandra.
            And I know you *think* that's important, but
            I don't. I think the reason he wasn't, is not
            here now, is because he didn't deserve you.

ALEXANDRA   But maybe I should be the one to decide
            that.

FRANK   Yes, maybe.

ALEXANDRA   This is messy.

FRANK   Yes.

ALEXANDRA   Did you ever sleep with her?

FRANK   Yes.

ALEXANDRA   OK. That was straight.

FRANK   But years . . . years before . . .

ALEXANDRA   When?

FRANK   It wasn't for long: round about the time
            of . . .

ALEXANDRA   Chalmers.

FRANK   Chalmers, yeah.

ALEXANDRA   God, he gets everywhere, doesn't he?

FRANK I think the experience was tough on your mum. She went on a bit of a run.

ALEXANDRA Bit of a run?

FRANK Yeah, men, you know.

ALEXANDRA Ugh. Naughty Mum.

FRANK I don't think she was enjoying it as such.

ALEXANDRA What a shame. I think I'm a bit scared, Uncle Frank.

FRANK That's good, Alexandra.

ISOBEL enters. It's clear she's been crying. She hands ALEXANDRA some money.

ISOBEL You don't need to go.

ALEXANDRA I do.

ISOBEL Don't go.

ALEXANDRA I'm going.

ISOBEL Leave Alfred Chalmers to me.

ALEXANDRA You want all the glory.

ISOBEL There's no glory to get.

ALEXANDRA Everything keeps being dragged back to then, to that time, doesn't it? *(Beat)* It's like a black hole. Even our home is not what it was. Or maybe for you it's not a dark hole at all. It's the light.

ISOBEL   I love you.

ALEXANDRA   *(Crying)* What did you do, Mum? What did you do?

ALEXANDRA leaves.

FRANK   I'll take her . . . Are you OK?

ISOBEL   I'm fine. Go.

FRANK   I could stay . . .

ISOBEL   No, go. Please go.

FRANK exits. ISOBEL sits, opens Sarah's file. She takes out a purse. A bracelet. Ring. She looks in the purse, takes out some coins, notes. She opens a bit of the purse and takes out receipts, three or four bus tickets.

ISOBEL   Did you collect bus tickets, Sarah? These are May, May, May, June – a whole three months before he took you. The 23. She took your bus route to university, Alexandra. She rode on your bus. Where did you go to, I wonder? Receipts: April, sandwich and a coffee; May, bowl of soup, a Marathon; May, sandwich and crisps. Student Union? You ate at the university. But you had a benefit card?

She checks all three receipts.

ISOBEL   You weren't really unemployed, were you,
          Sarah? You were a student. So why did no
          one . . . ? Because. Oh stupid stupid. Who
          wants their dead daughter's name in the
          papers for benefit fraud? You broke the
          pattern, Sarah. You weren't like the others.
          And we missed it.

SCENE FOUR

CHALMERS in the waiting room. He is nervous, tap-tapping.
JUDITH is there.

CHALMERS   Is that the right time?

JUDITH   Yes, Alfred . . .

ISOBEL is late. Finally she arrives.

CHALMERS   You're late. I can't abide it when—

ISOBEL   You've been in contact with my daughter.

CHALMERS   Oh. Yes, I have. Sorry.

ISOBEL   Sorry?

CHALMERS   What can I say?

ISOBEL   Well, what can *I* say?

ISOBEL gets up to leave.

CHALMERS   Wait. How was I to know you would turn up?

ISOBEL   You made contact with my daughter?

CHALMERS   It was an accident.

ISOBEL   Liar.

CHALMERS   You put me in here!

ISOBEL   Not interested. It's finished.

CHALMERS   I was going to string her along, probably
            let her do her documentary, feed her a few
            scraps. It gets publicity. Maybe it gets my
            case looked at! Shames you. Maybe messes
            up you and her just like you did to me.
            Revenge on you and yours. A bit nasty, but
            nothing compared to what you did to me!

ISOBEL   Oh, I don't know.

CHALMERS   What don't you know?

ISOBEL   Where it begins and ends with you, the
            truth, the lies; never did.

CHALMERS   What do you think I could have done,
            Isobel? I'm here! I'm an old man.

ISOBEL   I don't know.

CHALMERS   There's nothing else to know.

ISOBEL   I need some time.

CHALMERS   My time is on your hands, missy.

ISOBEL   And what's on yours?

CHALMERS   Less than you think.

ISOBEL   I don't think so.

CHALMERS   But you're not sure.

ISOBEL   No.

CHALMERS   Do you know something? *(Beat)* Suspect?
            Smell? Taste? An itch you can't get rid of?

ISOBEL   There's evidence missing. The fibre.

CHALMERS   Missing? How could that happen?

ISOBEL   I don't know.

CHALMERS   But what do you think?

ISOBEL   It could just have happened.

CHALMERS   Just happened? Chief Superintendent?
            Just happened.

ISOBEL   Happens.

CHALMERS   Does it?

ISOBEL   I was going to have it checked. Forensics
            has moved on.

CHALMERS   But now?

ISOBEL   Now I can't.

CHALMERS   Who knows you were talking to me?

ISOBEL   I told Black Fergus and Frank.

CHALMERS   Anyone else?

ISOBEL   No one. They were angry. They didn't
            understand.

CHALMERS   Oh, they understood.

ISOBEL   Fergus has had a stroke. I thought *I* caused
            it. But then . . .

CHALMERS   But then? Then you thought—

ISOBEL   I thought, what if it was guilt?

CHALMERS   I know about guilt, Isobel. I've always felt
            guilty, but not like you might think. Guilty
            that I was me. That I was who I was. I was
            cleverer than any of them but I could not
            make sense of why . . . why no one could
            find a way to like me. I was amazed when
            my wife agreed to accompany me to the
            pictures, then to dinner, took me to meet
            her parents. And then when she married me
            and had my daughter, I always felt like I'd
            be found out and they'd see I wasn't worth
            it. But I didn't deserve to lose them like
            I did. So when they abandoned me, as of
            course they would, that guilt was like I was
            burning. Not because of murder. But guilt at
            the inevitable misery of drawing them close
            to me and making them suffer.

ISOBEL   Your daughter never made contact?

CHALMERS   I suppose she must have read the
            headlines. Seen the pictures of me dressed
            in guilt – handcuffs and hoods. And then
            the pictures of those girls.

ISOBEL   The girls.

CHALMERS   I want to help you.

ISOBEL   Good.

CHALMERS   I want to help you get what you need.

ISOBEL   OK.

CHALMERS   That fourth victim.

ISOBEL   Yes?

CHALMERS   The one you nailed me on.

ISOBEL   Yes, I know.

CHALMERS   The other three just sat under the trial but with no evidence.

ISOBEL   You had no alibis.

CHALMERS   I'm not on trial again here. I'm trying to give you something, girl, so listen.

ISOBEL   Go ahead.

CHALMERS   Was there any connection with someone on the case – besides yourself – who might be seen to benefit from the death of that girl and my conviction?

ISOBEL   Well – I always knew it had helped my career.

CHALMERS   Just you?

ISOBEL   Fergus was made chief constable, but . . .

CHALMERS   But? And Frank? You don't have the answer
            because you've not done the thinking, so
            you need to go now and think. But you
            smell it, don't you? You know you got it
            wrong. I think you probably smelled it then.
            I think you did, didn't you?

ISOBEL   I thought you did it.

CHALMERS   And that's where it all went wrong and
            when the smell started.

ISOBEL   No alibis. It was you. We all sat and looked
            at the facts and it was you. All the girls had
            their abortions in your ward.

CHALMERS   And now?

ISOBEL   It was you.

CHALMERS   Why would I waste my time with a lie?
            Think. I want the sun. I also have a
            daughter somewhere out there cursed
            with what you, Black Fergus and Frank
            Bowman did to her. Something went wrong
            that night you arrested me, or before then.
            Halloween. Remember. Think back, and if
            you didn't do something, someone else did.

    ISOBEL gets up to go.

ISOBEL	She was a student. The fourth girl. All the other three were unemployed. She was different.
CHALMERS	*(Beat)* Was she?
ISOBEL	And what was the fox doing?
CHALMERS	The fox again?
ISOBEL	There was a fox. When he – you – took her eyes.
CHALMERS	What's a fox got to do with this?
ISOBEL	Don't know.
CHALMERS	Hold your nerve. Get the truth out before it rots you. Get the truth and write your book and I promise I'll leave Alexandra alone, never speak to her again. I'll refuse.
ISOBEL	I could stop that anyway.
CHALMERS	Could you? Youth, you know.
JUDITH	Time's up.
ISOBEL	I don't want you ever contacting her again.
CHALMERS	Of course. Isobel. Thank you. Don't feel guilty. Don't hate. Look where it got me.

ISOBEL exits. Voices off. CHALMERS sits for a while. He gets up and exits, JUDITH opening the door for him.

SCENE FIVE

ISOBEL enters. Drunk. Maybe with chips. Perhaps a sound of something as she enters. She tries to put the light on but it doesn't work. Tries several times. It is very dark and shadowy.

ISOBEL   Thanks. Thanks for that.

The answerphone light is flashing. She goes over, manages to press the right button.

ALEXANDRA   *(Voice from the answerphone)* OK, Mum, so you've managed to mess that up for me too. Tried calling him at the time we agreed but he was 'not available'. Got a message saying it was best we didn't 'proceed with our project'. My project. So you win. Well done you. Like always, Chief Superintendent McArthur. I'd say I hate you but then I'd sound like a teenager and I'd feel even more stupid, ridiculous and failing than I already do. I don't know what age I am any more. I'm thinking of leaving uni.

The dead tone tells us she has hung up.

ISOBEL   Good. Good.

> *Suddenly a person in a fox-head mask appears and attacks*
> *ISOBEL, hitting her several times with something, probably*
> *from the house. As ISOBEL lies still, groaning, the person*
> *grabs some of the files, photos, etc., and stuffs them into*
> *a holdall. ISOBEL crawls across the floor. She manages to*
> *get her hands on her mobile and starts dialling. FOXHEAD*
> *sees her, takes the phone from her, smashes it, pulls out*
> *the house phone from the socket. Looks as if there might*
> *be more violence visited on ISOBEL, but then FOXHEAD*
> *exits quickly. ISOBEL recovers, manages to drag herself up*
> *to the settee.*

ISOBEL   What am I doing? What have I done? *(She*
          screams, more in anger than anything else) Piece
          it together. Piece it together, Isobel. Man up!
          Come on. Man up! He comes here, gets in – or
          does he come in with her? – and kills her; he
          scrapes her eyes out, pours in the tar, puts the
          diamanté in but he doesn't place her in his
          constellation. You didn't do that.

> *CHALMERS appears or enters in the shadows, half seen.*

ISOBEL   Where are you?

CHALMERS Always where you want me to be. I'm in
          your house.

ISOBEL	Why did you leave her here?
CHALMERS	That'd be telling.
ISOBEL	Why did you hide her?
CHALMERS	Because she wasn't for showing.
ISOBEL	Not like the others.
CHALMERS	Didn't know that till after.
ISOBEL	Of course you didn't.
CHALMERS	What if I tell you I didn't do them all?
ISOBEL	Two killers?
CHALMERS	And I wasn't either of them.
ISOBEL	It had to be you. Alfred, the stars have all died out now. It's time to be honest. Did you kill her? Did you kill all those girls?
CHALMERS	Listen, just because this is your projection doesn't mean I'm still not cleverer than you are.
ISOBEL	Doesn't make sense and is impossible. Why bury her in her own house?
CHALMERS	Why not? Moving a body around can be difficult.
ISOBEL	You didn't want her to be found? No, you hid her. You were ashamed?

CHALMERS	You sent me down on an illusion. You worked it up between you, loved-up group of liars.
ISOBEL	It wasn't a stitch-up.
CHALMERS	Your drive is your weakness. When it heard the crowd cheering, it just went for it. You went for me. You got me.
ISOBEL	The fibres proved it.
CHALMERS	Oh, you mean the fibres that have gone walkies?
ISOBEL	*(Holding her arm and groaning)* I feel sick.
CHALMERS	Even now you give me indigestion on a meal I ate twenty-five years ago.
ISOBEL	You can't invent forensic evidence.
CHALMERS	No, but you can put it where it never should have been.
ISOBEL	Why?
CHALMERS	The story was too good not to be true. So you, or maybe Black Fergus or your boyfriend, Frank, made sure the narrative stuck.
ISOBEL	They're good cops. And he's not my boyfriend.
CHALMERS	A good cop doesn't create fictions, only facts. But you were too hungry.

ISOBEL   I wanted to stop the murders. They were
           alive when you took out their eyes!

CHALMERS   And hungry for Frank too – yes, gobbled
           him up just like you gob—

He spits out an eyeball that he has eaten.

CHALMERS   That's disgusting.

ISOBEL   I didn't mean that.

CHALMERS   Then why is it here? You're getting off on
           this too much.

ISOBEL   I only want the truth.

CHALMERS   Like I'm a piece of porn. A piece of porn you
           made. And maybe thought you shouldn't
           have. But love to watch.

ISOBEL   What's the fox head?

CHALMERS   The head of an animal.

ISOBEL   You've told me nothing.

CHALMERS   I've told you truths. Now excuse me whilst
           I enjoy the illusion of freedom in my past.

There is a sound off, like a door opening and closing.

CHALMERS   Her. Sarah. She's come home.

ISOBEL   No.

SARAH McELHENNEY enters the room. Sees CHALMERS,
who lunges at her. It is a terrible murder, messy and violent.

CHALMERS   Why are you making me do this?

ISOBEL   I'm not making you do it. Stop!

CHALMERS   It's already done!

SARAH   Jesus Christ, why did you let him do this?

ISOBEL   We tried to catch him! I'm sorry!

CHALMERS   You waste-of-space whore, cutting out life
            when you've no value. There's no light in
            you, none at all!

SARAH   You bitch, my mother's watching this.

ISOBEL   No she's not.

SARAH   She's always watching this.

ISOBEL   I want it to stop.

SARAH   How do you think I feel?

CHALMERS   I didn't do this!

He finds several bus tickets and a student card in his hand.

CHALMERS   You're a student. But that's wrong.

ALEXANDRA walks in wearing provocative nightwear.
She's horrified at the visioning her mother is doing.

ISOBEL   Dressed like a slut as usual!

ALEXANDRA   What is wrong with you?

ISOBEL   Alexandra, get out.

ALEXANDRA   *(Indicating murder)* What is all that about?

ISOBEL   I'm trying to find the thing that just lets me understand the—

ALEXANDRA   Well, I'm trying to have sex, if you don't mind. Oooooh, I feel weirdly horny. I'm finding this a wee bit of a turn-on. Is that wrong?

FOXHEAD appears again at window. ALEXANDRA goes to exit. CHALMERS sees her for the first time. They both stare at each other for a long moment.

CHALMERS   Sarah?

ALEXANDRA   Alexandra.

CHALMERS   I've made a terrible mistake.

ISOBEL   What mistake?

CHALMERS   I don't make mistakes.

ALEXANDRA   Is she dead?

CHALMERS   She doesn't fit into the sky.

ISOBEL   Doesn't she?

CHALMERS   I broke the truth of it. There's no pattern –
             no meaning.

ISOBEL   But then?

CHALMERS   *(To ALEXANDRA)* Sarah?

ALEXANDRA   I'm Alexandra.

CHALMERS   *(Indicates SARAH)* She's a student.

ALEXANDRA   Is she?

SARAH   Yes.

ALEXANDRA   Shouldn't you be dead by now?

CHALMERS   In a bit. *(Still to ALEXANDRA)* Sarah?

ISOBEL   Stop talking to her. She's my daughter.

ALEXANDRA   I was just having sex and I heard all this.

CHALMERS   I made a mistake. She's a student.

ALEXANDRA   I'm a student. We took the same bus, didn't
             we, Mum?

CHALMERS   You're a student too?

ALEXANDRA   Yes.

CHALMERS   Two of you. *(To SARAH)* Sarah? Sarah?
             (Beat) She's dead now. Look what you made
             me do.

ISOBEL   You must have done it.

CHALMERS   Did I?

ALEXANDRA   It's OK, we'll work it out.

ISOBEL   Stay away from him, Alexandra.

ALEXANDRA moves physically a little closer to CHALMERS.

ISOBEL   Oh please, my darling daughter. Oh please, Alexandra.

FOXHEAD appears in room.

ALEXANDRA   Aren't you going to make a constellation with her?

CHALMERS   She's only one. You can't make a constellation with only one star.

ALEXANDRA   That's true, Mum. Even I know that.

CHALMERS   You need two.

ISOBEL   I'm really really sorry and I love you.

FOXHEAD runs up to ALEXANDRA and places a knife at her throat, stays there panting for a while.

CHALMERS   This has nothing to do with me.

CHALMERS exits, dragging SARAH's body off. As soon as he has gone, FOXHEAD suddenly disengages and runs off. ALEXANDRA remains still.

ISOBEL   Are you all right?

ALEXANDRA picks a hair from her clothing where FOXHEAD had its face.

ALEXANDRA   Yes. Yes. I'd better go and finish the sex off now.

ISOBEL   You go and finish your sex off, my darling.

ALEXANDRA   OK, Mum.

ALEXANDRA exits.

ISOBEL   Facts. Facts, Isobel, facts. Four murders. Three unemployed women who'd had abortions. A student who'd had an abortion. Three displayed in a constellation, the other hidden. All four, tar-filled eyes and diamanté. A trick of yours to put us off? Or you made a mistake. Or was there a copycat who wanted to frame you? Or are you the fall guy and I drove it home because of bad maths? And you're innocent? And the fucking fox . . . ? *(Groans)* I'm trying, Sarah. I'm getting nearer. Stay with me. Oh dear God, I'm trying to see. I'm open to everything.

Blackout with ISOBEL sitting there.

SCENE SIX

FRANK and FERGUS in ISOBEL's office. Waiting. FERGUS in a wheelchair. His speech is impaired from his stroke.

FERGUS   Are you sure she is due in?

FRANK   Yes. Young Drew told me.

FERGUS   Everyone is young now.

FRANK   Right.

FERGUS   Apart from me.

FRANK   Right.

FERGUS   Do you think the stroke was a signal that old age is near?

FRANK   Fergus, the train passed that signal a wee while back!

FERGUS   Fuck . . . Do you love her?

FRANK   Probably. As much as I know what that bollocks means.

FERGUS   You just know it.

FRANK   OK then. *(Beat)* Fergus, don't take this wrong, but you talking about love with me . . . Let's stick to whisky, golf and crime, eh?

FERGUS   All right.

FRANK   Hope you don't mind.

FERGUS   Fuck you.

FRANK   Thanks.

FERGUS   Okey-dokey.

ISOBEL enters. Her arm is in a sling.

ISOBEL   Frank? Fergus?

FRANK   What happened to your arm?

ISOBEL   Fell off my bike.

FRANK   Didn't tell me.

ISOBEL   Should I have?

DREW enters.

DREW   The minister's special adviser is here.

ISOBEL   Is she? How did you and Detective Superintendent Bowman get on in the pub the other night?

DREW   Fine, ma'am.

ISOBEL   That's good then, Drew, that's good.

DREW   What will I tell her?

ISOBEL   Say I'll be right there.

DREW   How long?

FRANK   Just do it, son.

DREW exits.

ISOBEL Where were you last Thursday night?

FRANK   What?

ISOBEL Where were you?

FRANK   I don't know. At home, probably. Though not
        a Champions League night, so frankly could
        have been anywhere.

ISOBEL Right.

FRANK   Why?

ISOBEL Just wondered.

FRANK   Oh really.

ISOBEL I just wondered. *(With sudden briskness)* I need
        to get ready.

FERGUS Say what you are thinking.

ISOBEL Got the minister breathing down my neck.
        I'd better go.

FERGUS What do you think of Frank?

ISOBEL What does that mean?

FRANK   Yeah, what does—

FERGUS   Do you think he's a liar?

FRANK   Fuck's sake, Fergus.

FERGUS   What do you think he did? What's he covering up, Isobel?

ISOBEL   I'm making connections, but I don't know if they're real.

FERGUS   Then ask the questions.

ISOBEL   I don't know if I know what the questions are.

DREW re-enters.

DREW   That's them here, how—

ISOBEL   Five minutes.

DREW   Will I say—

ISOBEL   You'll say five fucking minutes, that's what you'll say.

DREW   Will do, ma'am.

DREW exits.

ISOBEL   I try to imagine how it was with . . . with the women who were killed.

FRANK   I thought you'd stopped doing that *Cracker* thing.

153

ISOBEL   And I keep seeing this . . . It's like a man in
         a fox's head, all bloody and terrible.

FRANK   This is something you imagined, yeah?

ISOBEL   You used to say my imagination and logic were
         friends when for most people they are enemies.

FRANK   I used to suck on my mother's nipples too, but
         not now!

ISOBEL   Frank, that is disgusting.

FRANK   I know, I don't know why I said that.

ISOBEL   You were making a point.

FRANK   I *was* making a point.

ISOBEL   It's OK.

FRANK   Is it?

FERGUS   All over again.

ISOBEL   What, Fergus?

FERGUS   Him. All over again. It's what he does.
         He's doing it again.

ISOBEL   Are you, either of you, hiding something from
         me? Is there something you have done that you
         don't want me to know?

FERGUS and FRANK hesitate.

ISOBEL   Oh God.

FERGUS   Don't think the worst.

ISOBEL   I was attacked Thursday night.

FRANK   Didn't know.

ISOBEL   Nobody knows. I wasn't at work. It was in my home.

FRANK   How—

ISOBEL   Don't know. I was drunk. I've been leaving the latch open just in case Alexandra . . . Only the person that attacked me had on a mask. A fox head. Not something I imagined. Real. Which is interesting because there are only two people I have mentioned this to and that is you, Frank, and Alfred Chalmers.

FRANK   You think I attacked you?

ISOBEL   Maybe not you. *(Looks in direction of the door)* I don't know.

FRANK   Yes you do.

ISOBEL   I don't.

FRANK   OK, fuck this. I'm a good man, Isobel.

ISOBEL   What did that good man do?

FRANK   I do the right thing. He did it. He killed those women.

155

ISOBEL   You know that?

FRANK   I'm saying those girls aren't here to speak for
          themselves now.

ISOBEL   And you speak for them, do you?

FRANK   Who do you speak for? For him? I am a messy
          human being in a very messy fucked-up planet
          and here is the thing I know best: that when
          I meet my God, I can look him in the face and
          say I tried to make the shit a little better by
          what I did. And I tell you, Isobel, I call it now
          and I say he's guilty and those girls were
          denied a life of love and mess because he cut
          them off. Good luck with your indulgent search
          for the truth.

FRANK starts to leave.

ISOBEL   You can't just walk away from this.

FRANK   This is as close to self-harming in police work
          as I've ever seen!

ISOBEL   Someone attacked me!

FERGUS   Tell her. *(FRANK stops)* Tell her.

FRANK   Fergus!

ISOBEL   Tell me what?

FRANK is silent.

FERGUS It was a Wolfman . . .

ISOBEL A what?

FERGUS The night we arrested him. It was Halloween, remember. The station had a party. And we all had masks on.

ISOBEL Did we?

FERGUS We did.

ISOBEL Oh my God. Did the fabric from one of the masks . . .

FRANK Maybe. *Maybe.*

ISOBEL What? It matched the fabric from her – Sarah's fur coat?

FRANK That's not the point!

ISOBEL Did someone put it on his jacket? And now that someone has decided to get rid of the evidence just in case a new forensics test would be damning.

FRANK No.

ISOBEL Well who did then, Frank? Who put the fucking mask on Chalmers' jacket?

FERGUS You did.

Silence.

ISOBEL   What?

FRANK   Jesus, Fergus.

FERGUS   You did.

ISOBEL   No, no. *(Beat)* No. *(Beat)* I can't . . .

FERGUS   It was you, Isobel.

FRANK   You put the mask on the mannequin. The
          mannequin had Chalmers' jacket on it. Waiting
          to be taken to Forensics. In a couple of hours it
          wouldn't have been there. It would have been
          in a lab. And then, yes, maybe history would
          have turned out differently. It was a moment,
          only a moment. The beast's head on the body of
          the beast. You laughed. And then we laughed.
          We were all drunk, elated and destroyed all
          at the same time and came in to look at him
          on the CCTV and feel good that no young
          woman out there would die that night. It was
          Halloween. And we had masks. And you were
          the Wolfman.

ISOBEL   No, no, I would remember that.

FRANK   I don't think it even occurred to us, to put the
          two together at the time.

ISOBEL   It didn't *occur*? Why can't I remember that?
          Why can't I remember what happened? What's
          wrong with me?

FERGUS   We care for you. And we were right to care for
          you.

ISOBEL   He needs to be freed.

FERGUS   Chalmers is a murderer.

ISOBEL   No, this confirms—

FRANK   Nothing. That fibre might not have come from
          the Wolfman mask. It might have been Sarah's
          coat.

ISOBEL   But we don't know that.

FRANK   It is possible.

ISOBEL   That's not our job.

FRANK   Kill the conversations with Chalmers, Isobel.
          Has Alexandra cut off from him?

ISOBEL   I've ended that. He just wants me. He thinks I
          can give him justice. Can I?

FRANK   That's been done.

ISOBEL   The only real evidence was a lie.

FRANK   Was *maybe* a lie.

ISOBEL   It was me.

FRANK   I've been doing a bit of work. I found out how
          he contacted Alexandra. It was fucking Twitter.

ISOBEL   But he can't have—

FRANK   But he has. So it looks like he's got a
         smartphone or access to a computer.

ISOBEL   Did you get rid of that strand of fibre?

FRANK   If I say no, will you believe me? If I say I did it.
         For you. Where would that leave you?

ISOBEL   That's not what we do. We just take the
         evidence and we act.

FRANK   We're here to get the bad guys. Whatever crisis
         is storming your sense of right and wrong, you
         need to get over it fast, or have you forgotten
         how much of a monster he is? You can't *change*
         that. You can't reinvent that.

FERGUS   Have I been struck down by God, Isobel?

ISOBEL   No, Fergus.

FERGUS   In my blacker Black Fergus moments, I don't
         know.

ISOBEL   You're a good man.

FERGUS   How do you know?

ISOBEL   Because I know.

FERGUS   Call Chalmers now, because you know it is the
         right thing. Because you *know*.

ISOBEL   Do I?

They sit in silence. She picks up her mobile and calls.

ISOBEL   Hello, Judith? *(Beat)* This is Isobel McArthur.
          (Beat) Yes, I wonder if you could relay a simple
          message to Alfred Chalmers. *(Beat)* Thanks.
          It is: 'There will be no more meetings. There
          will be no book. Nothing has changed.' *(Beat)*
          Yes, thank you. Bye.

FERGUS   Excellent access facilities here.

FRANK wheels FERGUS out.

ISOBEL   *(Calls off)* Janice?

JANICE enters.

JANICE   Ma'am?

ISOBEL   Get the tea and biscuits out. I'm ready.

JANICE   Will do.

ISOBEL sits in her chair and waits.

SCENE SEVEN

CHALMERS So dark and only four o'clock. Where's
Judith today?

MALE NURSE Called in sick.

CHALMERS Nothing serious, I hope?

*The YOUNG MALE NURSE exits. CHALMERS feels about
underneath the table, finds something and is satisfied.
The door of the waiting room opens and the YOUNG MALE
NURSE enters with, following him, ALEXANDRA.
CHALMERS is visibly excited.*

CHALMERS I never imagined . . . You are really here.

ALEXANDRA Yes. Here I am.

CHALMERS I know you must be nervous, but please
relax. You are the first new, sane person
I have met for over twenty-five years
who didn't want to either contain or
medicate me.

ALEXANDRA I don't want to do either of those things.

CHALMERS No, I know. I'm a little overwhelmed that
this has happened. I'm sorry if I let you
down, Alexandra, but your mother's book
could have seen me get justice and freedom.

ALEXANDRA I understand, but I needed to see you. How did you get your granddaughter's passport?

CHALMERS It's not real. I have found some rare advantages to my current society and their less than savoury networks and skills.

ALEXANDRA They wouldn't let me bring the recorder in.

CHALMERS Need to plan for that. Papers, et cetera, et cetera.

ALEXANDRA I feel I can look at you, and I know you can't be guilty.

CHALMERS How does that feel?

ALEXANDRA It makes me feel it was right to come here.

CHALMERS I think it was. How is your mother about this?

ALEXANDRA She doesn't know.

CHALMERS Ah.

ALEXANDRA She asked me to stop the contact.

CHALMERS And why didn't you?

ALEXANDRA Because I think there's something stuck back then for me too, like something lodged in the back of my throat. This could just sort things maybe for all three of us.

CHALMERS Well . . .

ALEXANDRA   Listen, Alfred, I don't want to put pressure
             on you, but *this* is the thing that's getting
             me through right now.

CHALMERS   Don't worry, what we're going to do will
             give you all the profile you need.

ALEXANDRA   And help you.

CHALMERS   And help me.

ALEXANDRA   Can't believe they didn't let me bring the
             recorder in.

CHALMERS   To see you so upset over a thing like that.

ALEXANDRA   Sorry, was that insensitive?

CHALMERS   No, but it reminds me of what freedom is.

ALEXANDRA   That's beautiful. Do you mind if I write that
             down?

CHALMERS   No, no – go ahead.

ALEXANDRA   *(Getting her notepad out)* I think what I want
             to do is start from your words, next time
             I come, maybe. Then I'll, like, visit where
             you grew up, where you lived at the time ...
             when you were arrested. Take some footage.
             But then I just want to listen to your words
             and see what pictures and music come to
             me so that it's not literal but poetic, so we
             create something where truth lives behind
             the eyes of facts. Does that sound OK,
             Alfred?

CHALMERS   It sounds powerful.

ALEXANDRA   It could be.

CHALMERS   It will need to be. You're probably my last
            chance. I never felt I had completed my
            statement of life, if you like.

ALEXANDRA   When I found out where . . . where I was
            living, I felt like *my* past was a lie.

CHALMERS   It was a mistake.

ALEXANDRA   No, it wasn't – how can you make a mistake
            like buying the house of the murder victim
            you were investigating?

CHALMERS   No, I mean I shouldn't have killed her. It
            was a mistake. She was a whore, but she
            hadn't one foot in the gutter.

ALEXANDRA   You did it?

CHALMERS   Oh yes.

ALEXANDRA   But . . .

CHALMERS   I know, I know . . .

*CHALMERS suddenly starts to choke. He doubles over
the table.*

CHALMERS   Nurse. Nurse.

165

*The **YOUNG MALE NURSE** rushes over to help him. In a*
second, Chalmers has him over the table and sticks a knife
*he procures from under the table into him. The **NURSE***
*slides to the floor. **CHALMERS** takes his keys from out of his*
pocket and locks the door, keeping the key in the lock.

CHALMERS   Do you have a fag?

ALEXANDRA   A what?

CHALMERS   A fucking fag, bitch, are you thick?

ALEXANDRA   I don't smoke.

CHALMERS   Fuck, doesn't smoke! Well, what will you
and I talk about now?

SCENE EIGHT

ISOBEL's living room is empty. ISOBEL enters and puts the lights on. She's on the phone. There is a real and bloody head of a fox in the living room. ISOBEL doesn't notice.

ISOBEL   . . . Please, Alexandra, just call. Love you.

She takes off her hat, maybe fires up the laptop. Finally she sees what we have all seen. She stops. At that moment a figure in a mask comes through the hallway door. ISOBEL makes to escape but the person pulls out a gun and points it at her.

ISOBEL   Who are you and what do you want? *(Beat)*
           Frank? Drew? Just take what you want
           and go.

The person takes off the mask. It is JUDITH, the young female nurse.

ISOBEL   You?

JUDITH   Sit down. Sit down!

ISOBEL does so.

ISOBEL   What now?

JUDITH   You'll see. Just wait.

ISOBEL   Is someone else coming?

JUDITH   Shut up.

ISOBEL   If you—

JUDITH   Shut up! Stop talking. I don't want you to talk.

ISOBEL   OK.

JUDITH takes out a mobile phone, texts and holds it in her hand. Waits.

ISOBEL   Whatever he told you, it's not true.

JUDITH   I know everything.

ISOBEL   He's manipulated you.

JUDITH   No, he's manipulated you. Silly cow.

ISOBEL   He manipulates everybody.

JUDITH   You're funny.

ISOBEL   I'm sorry if—

JUDITH   You should be sorry. He shouldn't be there.

ISOBEL   Oh yes he should.

JUDITH   *(As in panto)* Oh no he shouldn't. *(Beat)* You didn't get him. You cheated. You're a liar and a cheat. He had a family and—

ISOBEL   And Sarah McElhenney didn't?

JUDITH   He's a visionary. He had things to say.

ISOBEL   What were those things?

JUDITH   *(Remembering his words)* That we squander the
          life that's given us. That we abuse it. Make it
          empty. And then there's nothing. He needed us
          to wake up, to look up.

ISOBEL   There must be something wrong with the
          screening procedure at the unit. You're
          vulnerable.

JUDITH   *You're* vulnerable! I killed that fox. It's not easy
          to find a fox. You see them sometimes in the
          city. But when you want to kill one, it's not easy.
          Even the foxes don't know where they should
          be. They don't even know what they are any
          more. It's a mess. Never killed anything before.
          Had to keep it in my fridge. Yuck. Let me tell
          you, I've had to eat tinned food for the past five
          days. Still, worth it, though. You should have
          seen your face. *(Laughs)*

          *CHALMERS in the meeting room has taken out a phone and
          dialled.*

ISOBEL   It's not too late to—

          JUDITH's phone rings.

ISOBEL   Who's that?

JUDITH   You'll see. *(Answers)* Hello, Alfred.

CHALMERS   Hello, Judith. How are things your side?

JUDITH   They're fine.

CHALMERS   Good. Good.

JUDITH   Stay still!

ALEXANDRA   Who are you—

CHALMERS   Did I say you could speak?

JUDITH   Stop moving! Yours?

CHALMERS   All is well. *(To ALEXANDRA)* My colleague
            has someone there for you if you want to
            say a few words.

ALEXANDRA   Who?

CHALMERS   Put the phone on speaker now.

JUDITH   OK.

CHALMERS   It's your mum, Alexandra.

The phone speakers are both on now.

ALEXANDRA   Mum?

ISOBEL   Alexandra!

ALEXANDRA   Mum, he's killed a nurse and he's locked us
            in the room.

CHALMERS   That's enough.

ISOBEL	Alexandra, just do what he says. It'll be fine.
JUDITH	No it won't!
CHALMERS	Keep calm, Judith.
JUDITH	But she's—
CHALMERS	Stop getting excitable.
JUDITH	We've waited so long, Alfred, it's—
CHALMERS	Quiet! Isobel?
ISOBEL	Yes.
CHALMERS	It's good to meet your daughter. I hear she's moved out.
ISOBEL	Yes.
CHALMERS	No loyalty, eh?
ISOBEL	She's brilliant. She's becoming her own person.
CHALMERS	No, Isobel, you fucked up again. Just like you did all those years ago when you set me up.
ISOBEL	But you killed her.
CHALMERS	I know I killed her. I killed them all, of course I did that, but you didn't catch me.
ISOBEL	Then why are you there?

CHALMERS   Because of an injustice. Because of an
           ambitious young woman. I'm a bit flattered,
           though. I mean, to buy little Sarah's flat.
           No wonder your daughter's so needy.
           (To ALEXANDRA) Aren't you? Aren't you, girl?

ALEXANDRA   *(Crying)* Yes.

CHALMERS   Go on, say it.

ALEXANDRA   I'm needy.

CHALMERS   Again.

ALEXANDRA   I'm needy.

CHALMERS   Again.

ALEXANDRA   I'm needy.

ISOBEL   Please stop this, Alfred, there is nothing
           you can gain from it.

CHALMERS   That's not true.

ISOBEL   What can you gain that means anything?

CHALMERS   There isn't anything that means anything.

ISOBEL   It's not about the girls, it never was. This is
           about you. About you trying to give yourself
           meaning, isn't it? It's you that's needy, not
           my daughter.

CHALMERS   That's enough of your talking now, 'cause
           it's my turn and you don't spoil it for me!
           But you know, Isobel, for a little while I

thought you might actually get me out.
It did make me break my stride for a bit
on the Alexandra project.

ISOBEL   Please don't harm her. It's me you need to
take revenge on.

CHALMERS   Judith?

JUDITH   Yes.

CHALMERS   Shoot her.

JUDITH shoots ISOBEL in the leg.

ALEXANDRA Mum. Don't kill my mum, please.

ISOBEL   It's OK, Alexandra. I'm OK.

ALEXANDRA Mum!

CHALMERS   Already this feels better. Something real
is happening. And the good thing is that
probably no one will even try and get in
that door for the next twenty minutes.
So we can pretty much get through this
without any problems. You wronged me
and so I am going to wrong you. All those
useless girls, unemployed, killing their
babies after playing the slut, walking the
earth with no purpose. So I gave them a
purpose. I made them little stars. In the
constellation of the Vain Queen.

ISOBEL   You mutilated who they were.

CHALMERS   But when I made the mistake with that
            girl, I felt like I had betrayed myself, and
            her in a way. I had done my work, but then
            I found the student card in her pocket. I
            just wanted to hide her. But Isobel, you
            have made it perfect. Tonight I can finish
            my project. I can make a pattern. Sarah
            and Alexandra will always be spoken of
            together now. Because of you, they lived in
            the same house, their lives framed by the
            same walls, looked out the same windows
            and saw the same things; they took the
            same bus, they went to the same university.

ISOBEL   Oh Jesus Christ.

ALEXANDRA   Mum?

CHALMERS   I'm not going to kill you, Isobel, not your
            body. I'm going to make you look at my final
            pattern and forever see your dead daughter
            and know that you did it.

ALEXANDRA   Don't kill me.

CHALMERS   Don't be stupid: I've just told you the logic.
            Of course I'm—

FRANK   *(Over a speaker)* Alfred. Alfred? Alfred, we
            can see you. There's nowhere to go with
            this. Unlock the door and let us in.

CHALMERS   Is that you, Frank?

FRANK   Yes, it's Frank Bowman.

CHALMERS   You going to watch? *(Laughs)* Is Fergus there too?

FRANK   No, Fergus is not here.

CHALMERS   That's a pity. How did you turn up?

FRANK   That doesn't matter. What matters—

CHALMERS   You don't fucking tell me what matters, that's finished, so you just answer my questions now or I start cutting her eyes out.

ISOBEL   Frank!

FRANK   Some idiot forgot to tell me your 'granddaughter' was visiting. Thought it didn't matter.

ALEXANDRA   Uncle Frank, he's going to kill me. He said he's going to kill me.

FRANK   I won't let that happen.

CHALMERS   You're not in control here, sonny. Bitch is dead and a star is born.

JUDITH   The world will see him like the genius he is again.

CHALMERS   Shut up, Judith, just watch McArthur.

JUDITH	I shot her in the leg, Alfred, she's not going nowhere.
CHALMERS	Watch her. I don't want you messing this up.
JUDITH	I won't mess it up, I told you I wouldn't.
FRANK	That your real daughter, Chalmers?
CHALMERS	Just a fan, Frank.
ISOBEL	She's a psycho bitch, Frank, she's shot me in the leg.
FRANK	There are people on the way, hang in there.
JUDITH	Who? Who are on the way?
CHALMERS	Shut up and keep your mind on the job.
ISOBEL	If you run now, Judith, you might just make it. A few minutes more and you're ours.
JUDITH	That's not the plan. Can I shoot her, Alfred?
CHALMERS	No!
JUDITH	I shot the fox.
CHALMERS	Don't shoot her!
ALEXANDRA	Mum. Mum, I love you. I'm sorry, Mum. I'm really sorry.
ISOBEL	It's OK, baby. It was all me.
JUDITH	What do I do, Alfred?

CHALMERS   Stick to the plan!

JUDITH   She's looking at me funny. Stop looking at me, bitch.

ALEXANDRA   Mum, stop looking at her!

CHALMERS   Isobel, shut up or it starts now.

FRANK   Give it up, Chalmers.

ISOBEL   You're not him.

JUDITH   Then who am I? *(ISOBEL stands up)* Sit down!

CHALMERS   Do her other leg.

ISOBEL   Get out of here, Judith. Run!

JUDITH   I can't.

ISOBEL   You can.

JUDITH   I can't.

ISOBEL   Run, Judith, run.

JUDITH   I've nowhere to run to. There's nothing.

She shoots ISOBEL. There's a silence.

FRANK   Isobel? Isobel?

ALEXANDRA   Mum?

CHALMERS   Did you shoot her leg?

JUDITH   No.

CHALMERS   What?

JUDITH   I did it.

CHALMERS   What? Fucking bitch, what?

JUDITH   Right in the heart. She's all gone.

*CHALMERS makes a choice and starts moving towards the
screaming ALEXANDRA.*

FRANK   Alexandra, Alexandra . . . Alex, can you
            hear me?

CHALMERS sits down, disengaged.

CHALMERS   It's dark.

FRANK   Alexandra?

ALEXANDRA   I'm so sorry.

FRANK   Unlock the door . . . let me in.

ALEXANDRA   I want my mum . . . I want my mum . . .
            I love her.

FRANK   It's going to be OK . . . unlock the door.

ALEXANDRA   I love her.

Blackout.

IAN RANKIN and MARK THOMSON

In conversation with the Lyceum's Michelle Mangan

How did Dark Road come about? Who approached who and when did you set about writing the piece?

Ian: I'm fairly sure the original question came from Mark during coffee and chat. Why do we see so many cop shows on TV and so few on the stage? He challenged me to come up with a story that was properly dramatic and meaty. I went away, thought about it, and offered him a few scenarios. He chose the one he felt best suited the stage, and a company of great actors.

Mark: Yes, I definitely was the suitor! And I knew Ian loved the theatre as I often see him at the Lyceum. I think he is one of our great storytellers and I was very intrigued to find a way to get him on our stage in a genre that is celebrated more in novels, TV and film.

Can you give us an insight into the writing process and how you found collaborating together?

Ian: Having storyboarded the play and delineated the main characters, I left it to Mark to write the dialogue. He provided a structure that really worked and we began to bounce ideas, rework dialogue and research back and forth, meeting to go through the script in detail until we had something we could offer actors – roles we felt would challenge and excite them.

Mark: Ian story, me dialogue, allowed us to get to know and trust each other. But there is Rankin dialogue in the play as well as plot developments that emerged once I started to write the dialogue. We spent a great deal of time tuning into each other. For example (I'll mention the R word here), we did talk about Rebus but quickly dismissed it as a predictable choice – he already exists both on the page and screen. I think we were clear that constructing a story from scratch, that would be best told on stage, was our ambition.

When it came to casting, did you both have a say in that?

Ian: From the word go, Mark had Maureen Beattie in mind and I left the casting decisions to him – he is the expert, after all! But I've been thrilled by the way rehearsals have gone, the ensemble spark off each other in ways I hadn't imagined.

Mark: Yes, ultimately it's the director's job to cast but I always ask playwrights' views. Is there anyone comes into their head? We bounced ideas about, mostly to come to some sense of the kind of animal we were looking for. Then I got on with it. And now we have a room that is a lively mix of great experience and terrific young talent, all united in intelligence and generosity.

Ian, how have you found the experience of writing for the stage and how did you feel in the rehearsal room watching your characters come to life?

Ian: The initial few days of read-throughs were interesting in themselves, but when we moved to rehearsals it got even better. Seeing the stage design was an amazing moment, too. It really is very special and solved some problems we had with the structure of the piece. Never having been in a theatre workshop environment, it's been a real privilege to see the actors begin to inhabit their roles. I've been put on the spot a few times, too. The characters in my books don't often turn to me and say 'I'm not really sure what's happening here'! Or there will be a query about procedure. One headache has been the reorganisation of Police Scotland – the play was written before the changes that took place in April 2013. Maureen's character has gone from being a chief constable (in the original draft) to a chief superintendent – as a direct result of the reorganisation.

Tell us a bit about the main themes of the play and give us an insight into your characters.

Ian: It's a psychodrama, I suppose, but also very firmly about family – the family you have at home, and the family your colleagues become when you join the police force. Isobel begins to wonder what she has lost as a result of climbing the greasy pole, and also suspects that her whole career has been constructed from a lie. I'd happily give more away than that, but Mark would probably kill me . . .

Mark: Yes, we don't want any famous writers being bumped off, that would be a terrible shame! I think Ian's highlighted the world of the play and I think our relationship with our own past is very strong in it, too. What was so vivid and inspiring was Ian's creation of the protagonists. Even the names resonated immediately. I mean, 'Black Fergus'! Who else but Ian could create him? You just know there's this creature hewn from the grey, unyielding Calvinist walls of our most austere churches.

Any stories you want to share from the rehearsal room?

Ian: Having spent a week and a bit in rehearsal, I then had to head off to Cape Town, so Mark probably has more stories than I do. But as someone who has often visited the theatre, but never been allowed behind the scenes until now, I've been fascinated by the stuff I've not been aware of, such as how to make entrances and exits. The actors will ask, 'Is this door going to open inwards or outwards?' And they need to know, of course. There is a real sense of detailed choreography and if that occasionally goes wrong in rehearsal, it allows for some laughter.

Mark: What happens in rehearsals stays in rehearsals! I suppose one thing I would say is that when you're doing something that has a real nastiness, real emotional pain and horror, then it's important to keep laughter high. You can't just stare and stare at the awfulness or you'll lose perspective.

As rehearsals have progressed, have you discovered any new elements in the play that weren't in your original vision?

Mark: Not new elements, no, but the journey of rehearsals can often mean that a scene has something under it that you didn't realise. The biggest thing in doing a crime piece is that we must make sure it adds up. Ambiguity and doubt are vital to the pleasure of seeing something like this, but it must be precise. And also the actors must keep their integrity always and never just play something because it helps create a useful doubt. Every action and thing that's said must come from somewhere real and honest.

Has the play changed during the rehearsal process?

Ian: While I was in South Africa, Mark sent me an email saying: 'No biggie, but I've just changed the order of a couple of scenes.' He explained the reasoning and I agreed with his decision. The actors are also chipping in, suggesting changes in phrasing to match their characters' personalities, or finding humour, by use of a facial expression or gesture, that elevates a moment in a scene.

Mark: I think what Ian mentions was the most significant – a little restructuring in the first half. The rest has been about cutting and fine-tuning rather than overhaul. However, the journey with how you play a scene may well shift quite radically. What you thought might work turns out to give the game away. So we all make character choices that help us construct this – what Barrie Keeffe called 'a pyramid of cards' – where if one card is out of place the whole bloody pack could come crumbling down. So we're placing them carefully!

Would you both do it again?

Ian: Would I write for the theatre again? Ask me when the Edinburgh run has ended!

Mark: Well, I've loved the process with Ian. He's been amazingly cool about entering this very collaborative world. As he says, as a novelist he sits in front of his computer and what he says goes, right from the story choices to whether the sun is out, or a character cries, is staring at another or sitting in a chair. Now he's thrown in with all of us collaborating over everything. Not one storm-out! Quite the opposite, in fact. I think he got the bug and enjoyed the buzz of having a set of sparky creative people in a room, hell-bent on finding the best way to tell his story.

THE CONVERSATION CONTINUES

Ian Rankin and Mark Thomson on *Dark Road*

Ian: Mark, my memory is that *Dark Road* started life almost as a dare – the question being: would a contemporary cop drama work on stage? Is that how you remember it?

Mark: Yes. I think it really started when you did a talk at the Lyceum on my production of James Hogg's *Confessions of a Justified Sinner*. I'd say we first bonded over literature and one of the greatest crime novels ever written. But then a few lunches later I remember us wondering how the crime genre might work on stage. I mean, I know there are Agatha Christies, but how possible was it to satisfy the fun and tension of a modern crime novel such as Ian's? Then the dare . . .

Ian: When I first pitched the plot to you, I think the central character was male. But you had a particular actor in mind, and asked if we could have a woman chief of police instead – and that totally changed the dynamic! Fortuitously so, I now think! Do you agree?

Mark: Yes, I remember that. Strange, because of course now you can't imagine it being a man. It's absolutely the story of an extraordinary woman in extraordinary circumstances. I did think, too, that getting away from Rebus would be healthy and interesting for you. A new adventure! And yes, I definitely suggested that there were a number of very strong Scottish actresses that would reward the piece, namely Maureen.

Ian: How would you describe the play? I've found myself calling it a drama of mind games and sexual politics. There is a whodunit element, too, of course . . .

Mark: I absolutely agree with that. I remember us talking about the tone and content. It had to celebrate your voice on stage. People were going to come and they would want to see your dark stories with vivid characters, twists and tensions. But OK, how would I describe our play? I think it's the story of a woman at a critical point in her life, needing to revisit the past before she can move, in any sense, to her future. The play is about the difficulties of finding truth in the past because you're not there. You're here and now. It's also the story of a mother and daughter.

Ian: Writing a play is one thing, but getting it ready for the stage is quite another matter. How traumatic was that?

Mark: Well, without sounding melodramatic, I always feel like it is a real cocktail of pragmatism and intense creativity. Every choice – whether it's casting, set, composer – starts to define and determine what the evening can be. It's full of fear and excitement. But I like all that. Who wants to do anything you don't care enough about to fear its failure?

Ian: After the first preview, you made a couple of big decisions, cutting one scene and lessening the body count at the end. As a newbie, it amazes me that this is possible – and that all those changes worked!

Mark: I think they did, Ian. It's the most I think I have ever changed over previews. But that was about us figuring out what worked and what didn't work regarding the crime drama. I remember needing more whisky than Rebus when I got home every night! But what was terrific and very lucky is that I always felt we travelled together. When things don't work and you have co-authors, then that can be tricky.

Ian: It seems to me that the set design solved quite a few potential problems, by being flexible as well as completely stunning. How important is it to you that theatre be immersive?

Mark: Entirely. I always say that the evening has to take the audience on a journey that is unpredictable and interesting. And the set had to do quite a lot of that work. Francis O'Connor is brilliant at taking care of how to find a physical articulation of story and create pleasing acrobatic solutions to whatever a play throws at him. We needed people to get lost in our dark world and not let them out till the house lights went up. The set, and of course the lights and music, all drew people in and sustained that tension.

Ian: Of course, with such complex staging, there must have been many potential pitfalls. Did you have any problems with it?

Mark: Well, the set was a revolve that had the three different locations on it. In the centre of it was a kind of weirdly shaped mini-room where most of the quick changes took place. During one show, poor Maureen was changing in one corner of it. But it was the wrong corner. Jo, our dresser, suddenly realised there was a wee section of the audience enjoying a view of Maureen in a state of undress that was definitely not required in the play, and had to howk her away.

Ian: The audiences were huge – I struggled to get a ticket some nights! And many of those people hardly ever went to the theatre. So do you think we proved our point with *Dark Road*?

Mark: Yes, we did. We made people jump. We entertained them. We kept them guessing. And the bar sales tell me that once we'd had our way with them, they needed a good bloody drink. I'm happy with that.

BEHIND THE SCENES

with Jo Rush
Assistant director at the Royal Lyceum Theatre Edinburgh

In the run-up to *Dark Road*'s opening night, assistant director Jo Rush kept a weekly rehearsal-room diary charting the play's journey from page to stage . . .

August 26th 2013
Today is the day that rehearsals for *Dark Road* officially begin.

I have personally been excited for this day since March and now that it's finally here I can't quite believe it.

Over the last five months, since I became assistant director to Mark Thomson, who has co-written this play with Ian Rankin, there has already been a huge amount to do before reaching this stage where at last we have actors, scripts and production team all in one rehearsal room together.

As an assistant director, my role is to support Mark's direction and provide a second opinion and sounding board for his ideas at all stages of the production, which gives me an amazing insight into how the play is put together.

As Mark has also written the script, an extra perspective is really helpful. In the build-up to starting rehearsals my role has entailed script reading, research, design meetings, casting, photo shoots and a surprising amount of secrecy.

Dark Road will be a world premiere for the Lyceum and the first time that Ian Rankin has written for the stage, so when I first found out that I would be working on the production I couldn't even tell anyone what the play was as it hadn't yet been formally announced.

And even now that the play is out in the public eye, the nature of the piece demands a certain level of caution when discussing it. Unlike many productions of classic plays with well-known plots, *Dark Road* is entirely new and needs to remain a complete surprise for the audience so they can best feel its impact. I would hate to deprive anyone of the feeling of exhilaration and confusion I had when I first hurtled to the conclusion of the play, so I'm being very careful not to give any spoilers!

I've worked with new writing previously at the Traverse where I have been an assistant director to Orla O'Loughlin and also directed at their Words, Words, Words new playwriting events so by now I'm used to reading various drafts of scripts with an eye out for confusions and inconsistencies and making sure the script flows.

For this collaboration, Ian has created the characters and content of the play and Mark has provided its dramatic shape and it is fascinating to see how enmeshed their writing has become. The play has a distinct, familiar Rankin flavour that sits perfectly within Mark's great ability to build drama and pace.

What makes Ian's work so recognisable and so perfect for the Lyceum is the way it is embedded in the geography of Scotland and particularly of Edinburgh. The familiarity of local monuments and street names is disrupted and disturbed by the crime scenes and bodies that his writing confronts you with.

I've enjoyed watching as these details become clearer in each draft of the script and couldn't quite stop myself shuddering uneasily as I read the latest draft and realised one of the murder victims lived just around the corner from me.

The work done in the last few months has given a series of teasing tastes of what this production will become. I've been able to see how the world of the play will look on stage by attending design meetings where the whole stage is shrunk to model size by the designer before being built for real by the Lyceum team at Roseburn.

I've spent the day worrying tourists and locals as we took photos of 'murder victims' in locations around the city to create crime-scene images – it seems only one person called the police on us! In casting meetings I've heard accomplished actors reading sections of the text and been given a tantalising glimpse of its potential.

And I've learnt far more than I ever expected to know about secure unit hospitals and police interview tape recorders.

But now, on day one of rehearsals, it's as simple as: one rehearsal room, eight actors, one director, one stage manager, one amazing script – and me.

And I can't wait to see it come to life.

September 3rd 2013

Getting to know you: Week one on the Royal Lyceum's *Dark Road*

After the months of waiting, somehow the first week of rehearsals for *Dark Road* has already sped by and it's suddenly September already.

We've had a brilliant week of getting to know each other and getting to grips with the complexities of the script. And it all began with day one and our first impressions.

You can never recreate a first impression. When working with a script the first reaction you have on reading it is often the closest you can get to what the audience will eventually experience so it's really important to pay attention to these impressions and ideas before becoming too familiar with the play.

Ian Rankin, Jo Rush and Mark Thomson during rehearsals.
Photo © Dan Travis, deputy stage manager, Royal Lyceum Theatre

We spent the first day and a half of our rehearsals going through the play scene by scene and seeing what questions were raised at the end of each scene. This was really valuable time for all of us as the crime thriller genre demands a clarity of storyline and plotting that we had to ensure made sense.

We were lucky enough to have Ian Rankin present in rehearsals with us for the whole of last week before he jetted off to a book festival in South Africa. Ian has been a great help whenever clarification of the story has been needed, particularly of unseen or secret parts of the plot that never appear on stage. And it's been really enjoyable to get an insight into his first impressions of rehearsing a stage play; being surprised by how many questions the actors asked and the different storytelling tools available in plays compared to novels.

'There's all these internal things going on that you can write in a novel but you don't have them on stage'

Ian Rankin

Ian and I have both been figuring out the best way to contribute in the rehearsal room. As assistant director there is no hard and fast rule to define my role in the rehearsal process; I'm there to support the director in whatever way is needed, which necessarily changes depending on the director you're working with. Ian, as a co-writer, and especially one who is working so closely with the play's director, is in a similar position.

Some writers are never in rehearsal, others choose to be there all day, every day, and involved in every

decision about the play. Ian has been striking a great
balance between the two: finding the right time to
give rewrites, not interrupting the flow of rehearsals,
but there to provide help and clarity when needed.
As a result, the cast have felt really encouraged by his
supportive attitude and 'benevolent presence' in the
room and have felt able to voice any questions they
have, which is key to the next phase of rehearsals
we entered into.

Asking the right questions – actually, just asking
any questions, no matter how silly they may sometimes
sound – is vital in the first week of rehearsals. You have
to throw ideas around and play with a lot of different
possible meanings without landing on answers at this
early stage. It's as simple as just trying stuff out and
using a process of elimination – every idea you reject
gets you closer to the right answer.

'Can you do it like Dennis Hopper in *Apocalypse Now*?'
Mark Thomson (to young *female* actor)

Because of this, lots of suggestions get thrown out
there that are designed to help the actors explore what
subtext is underlying each scene and from that point to
see how much it's actually possible to play.

You may decide that a character has a chronic fear
of light switches due to an electric shock received
at their third birthday party but can you play that
without having to just tell the audience? Or do you just
show that they never switch on the lights? Sometimes
actually all you can play is what's written, what the

characters say or do. But you have to ask questions first before you can know this for sure.

One of the more hilarious suggestions we encountered this week was whether or not our heroine would have a 'vajazzle' – we quickly decided that of course she wouldn't – but not before an awkward conversation where the exact definition of a vajazzle had to be explained to Mark . . . !

As we progressed through the first week and became more in tune with the play and its characters we found that the answers to our questions came more easily, but there is still a lot of exploration to be done. The richness and intrigue of this play lies in its complex characters and their relationships with one another and the fact that sometimes their actions are confusing even to themselves and can't be rationalised by us or by an audience, they simply act first and think later. And all of that is part of the story we have to tell.

Educating Ian:

Ian – 'It's funny how she mentions her three hundred and sixty-three followers on Twitter.'

Me – 'But that's because to us mere mortals that's actually loads! We can't all have sixty-two thousand followers!'

September 9th, 2013

Learning the walk: Week two on the Royal Lyceum's *Dark Road*

Getting the show on its feet so that the characters move and inhabit the world of the play has been the next stage of our rehearsal process for *Dark Road*.

It sounds so simple. Step 1: actor delivers line; step 2: actor moves around stage; step 3: actor combines moving and speaking *at same time* – and there you have a fully realised stage production!

But thankfully it is far from being this straightforward and the kind of stilted productions caused by this oversimplified attitude towards staging are a rare mistake.

Just as we have subjected the script to intense questioning and played with the options available to us, we have also approached the movement of the characters in this manner.

> Anonymous actor – 'You know when you start questioning yourself and you forget how to walk?'

You have to examine the impulses and energy of each character to find the way in which they should move in the stage space, asking the easy questions of 'Where do they need to be and when?' and also the more complex questions of motivations and reactions: 'How do they respond physically to other people?'; 'How comfortable do they feel in this particular setting?'

Rather than fix on set movements from A to B at this stage in rehearsal, Mark has encouraged the cast to move freely within the space in order to find what

works and what doesn't. Although some decisions –
such as which door a character enters through – need
to be made to make sense of a scene, on the whole, it's
not helpful to get weighed down in staging movement
too early.

If you do so, it can drain the playfulness and energy
of a rehearsal and prevent the actors from fully
exploring the dynamic and meaning of a scene because
they are focused on where they need to move, when.

Walking and talking at the same time may sound
fairly uncomplicated, but when you're asking an actor to
speak and to move in a psychologically believable way
for the character that they are playing, you are asking
a huge amount of them and it's easy to over-think this,
which is why it's best not to get bogged down in it while

Walking the walk in the rehearsal room.
Photo © Dan Travis, deputy stage manager, Royal Lyceum Theatre

vital work on the heart of the story and characters is still ongoing.

In my role as assistant director, one of the ways that I have been best able to contribute to the production has been in creating a precise timeline for the play's events. To do this I sat down with the script and went over it in detail for any reference to when events happen, how much time passes between one scene and the next, and what events happen in between scenes that we don't see on stage.

As the play takes place over several months in 2013 but also includes events that occurred in 1988, it can be difficult to keep track of the order of events. For the actors this is crucial as they need to understand what their character has experienced and knows at each point in the play to inform their character decisions for each scene.

The actors have to forget the full context and storyline of the play that they are aware of as actors and only respond to what their character knows at any given point so they are able to create a truthful reaction to the events their character experiences.

Being given definitive control over the play timeline has let out all my worst pedantic tendencies, earning me the nickname 'Timeline Fascist'. But having a very specific timeline is also so useful in making sure that all elements of our plot make sense and for the design team who can change clothes and lighting according to the time of year it is in the play. For me, it gives me a real feeling of connection with the events of the play and an understanding of it. Tomorrow morning, my timeline is going up on the rehearsal room wall for all the company to see and, despite the unfortunate dictator-associated nickname, I (not-so-secretly) love being a 'Timeline Fascist'!

September 16th 2013
Dark comedy: Week three on the Royal Lyceum's *Dark Road*

It's fair to say that Ian Rankin and Mark Thomson's first play together is not exactly a light-hearted farce – many apologies to anyone whose expectations have now been shattered. And yet the presiding theme of our third week of rehearsals has been laughter.

Maybe it's the pressure from the ever-approaching deadline of first night, or perhaps it's the tension that builds up when you're rehearsing intense, dramatic scenes simply finding a way to be released. Either way, it's always the most serious scenes that are creating the most hilarity – with the steeliest of actors and directors reduced to fits of giggles by a surly-sounding secretary or an unyielding prop.

There are several benefits to a rehearsal room full of laughter, besides the obvious fact that it's a lot of fun. A company that are having a laugh and sharing in-jokes with each other is usually a well-bonded company. When you're spending so much time together it's a blessing if you can enjoy joking around and it boosts the morale and trust of the team, especially as you develop jokes that are personal to the show.

A particular source of entertainment in the company comes from suggestions of what would feature in *Dark Road: The Musical* with actors (and even our director) sometimes unable to resist the temptation to burst into a song and dance.

In a strange way, as you rehearse through each scene of the play it's really good for the actors to get any accidental funny moments out of their system so that they don't get thrown by them at a later date and end up dissolving with laughter mid-performance.

The particular challenge that we've been facing in *Dark Road* is how to allow for select moments of humour within the play but avoid unintentional humour at all

Director Mark Thomson in musical theatre mode.
Photo © Dan Travis, deputy stage manager, Royal Lyceum Theatre

costs. The last thing that anyone wants is a moment or phrase that seems too clichéd, innuendo-laden, or silly and raises a titter from the audience that destroys the drama of a scene. So we have to watch out along the way and flag up anything that might illicit an undesirable audience-chuckle.

Now that we're fully into the process of finalising the play's shape, seeing how each scene will look and what movements and moments will tell the story best, we are also adding in more props and costume to rehearsals. This is exciting as it fleshes out the look of the play, bringing us closer to seeing what its final appearance will be like.

Props are often not an actor's best friend. It may seem simple to open a cassette player, place a tape inside and press play. But, under the pressure of a performance and with lines, movements and timing to remember, it's surprising how easily those things can go wrong. Through practising the movements and action of each scene and using props as repetitively as possible throughout the rehearsal process the cast can build up their muscle-memory which will allow them to move without having to think about it and result in an action that appears natural in performance.

With more props in the room comes more opportunity for hilarity and (temporary) confusion. The cast have particularly enjoyed spinning round and round on the egg chair that features in the set, berating an imaginary secretary via telephone handset, and discussing how best to achieve a grotesque-looking eyeball. And our

sincere hope is that all of the many things that could
go wrong with props go wrong now in rehearsal rather
than during the run . . .

Two of our cast members, Maureen Beattie and Phil
Whitchurch, have already been experiencing show-related
nightmares, which at present mostly centre on the horror
of finding yourself in the middle of a scene with no idea of
what the lines are or even what the scene is.
    I was initiated into the nightmare-club myself on
Friday last week when I dreamt that, having missed
a day of rehearsals, I came back to find that the entire
story had been relocated to America and turned into
a cheap melodrama (complete with a tearful pregnant
woman arriving on someone's doorstep in the pouring
rain – I've no idea who she was!).
    I woke up absolutely raging that the exciting,
Edinburgh-based play I'd waited so long to see come to
life would never be put on the stage. You can imagine
the relief I felt when I realised that it was all in my
imagination.

Company illness of the week:
Metaphor fatigue – the loss of ability to express anything
via an appropriate verbal metaphor, symptomatic of
end-of-week-three-itis and evidenced by a string of
unrelated nouns and verbs jumbled together and ended
with a sigh. E.g. 'when there's – but you're reaching –
for the thing – the goal – and you still gather the cake.'

September 24th, 2013

Staggering through: Week four on the Royal Lyceum's *Dark Road*

The fourth week of rehearsals for *Dark Road* has seen us make the biggest transition of our rehearsal process so far – out of the rehearsal room and into the theatre. Hopefully the experience won't prove as traumatic as the proverb that phrase is riffing on!

Having spent four weeks in the rehearsal room – which is over the road from the theatre itself – we had all become comfortable in that familiar environment and the theatre space had started to feel strangely distant, to me at least. But with the beginning of week four reality hit with a bump – the set was not only fully built but already being assembled in the theatre and the Lyceum's excellent team of lighting, sound and technical crew were preparing for our arrival. Were we ready?

On Monday, while still in the rehearsal room, we attempted our first 'stagger through'. This is a fairly self-descriptive name used for the first time you run the play all the way through from beginning to end. Whereas you might call this a full 'run' of the play, describing it as a 'stagger' shows an awareness that everyone is doing this for the first time and are unlikely to be able to run before they can walk.

For the cast it is a particularly interesting experience to put all the scenes in order for the first time and see what stories are being told in the scenes that they don't appear in and how different plot lines sit next to each other in the body of the play. On the technical side, it was an opportunity for our lighting designer, Malcolm, to see the shape of the play, to see where the actors are moving and how they're using the set so that he can plan how best to light the show and get as many of those lights set up in the theatre ahead of our arrival.

Stage management, wardrobe, and our designer Francis also watched the stagger-through with a view to where changes could be made and how to plan for the smoothest possible working of the final show. It's safe to say there was a high level of concentration in the room which, when combined with the tense nature of the play, left us completely wiped out afterwards.

Working on a brand new play usually means that adjustments are being made to the script until very late in the process. Previous new plays that I've worked on have even been subject to rewrites after their first previews! Keeping track of the many changes to the script along the way and making sure that a master copy of the script is kept up to date has been one of the tasks that myself and Dan, our wonderful deputy stage manager, have been grappling with on a daily basis. It's so important to have a record of all the changes to the text because this will be the reference point for all the complicated cueing of lights, sound, and everything else so it needs to be as accurate as possible.

Bizarre moment of the week: having returned to us from South Africa, Ian – ever the most culturally savvy in the room – seemed to particularly enjoy explaining to two younger members of the company what 'twerking' is!

After Monday's stagger-through Mark went away and

made some cuts to the script to ensure that it would run at a good length on the stage and so on Tuesday we had to quickly take on these cuts and work with the actors whose lines were affected to get them used to the edits. Although it's occasionally sad when the play loses a particular phrase you've grown attached to, most of the cuts have simply helped us to avoid saying the same thing twice, or introducing information tangents that aren't needed in a scene, so the play now flows even better as a result.

After this, the bulk of our fourth week was all about repetition, repetition, repetition. Going over scenes again and again to get them built into the cast's muscle-memory and giving extra time to scenes or sections that caused difficulties to the actors so that they could overcome any problems and hone the scene through consistent practice.

By lunchtime on Friday we were ready to run! We had a proper full run of the show that afternoon in the rehearsal room with the whole production team watching and the difference that those four days had made was remarkable. With that done there was only one thing left to do – pack up our props and set and move into the theatre.

And that's where we've been for the last few days. Getting used to our new home, trying to understand the intricacies of the set, seeing costume, set, lighting and sound all finally come together. There's a lot that is still to be figured out before opening night but it's going to be amazing to see it get there through this final push.

September 25th, 2013

All tech-ed up: The final week on the Royal Lyceum's *Dark Road*

The final week leading up to our official opening night of *Dark Road* has been surreal to say the least. During tech week everyone essentially lives at the theatre all day, every day.

You start to lose touch with the outside world – and find it hard to explain to any friends who manage to make contact with you why you are so sleep-deprived and oversensitive!

The job of tech week is to bring together the full technical elements of the show: set, lighting, sound, projection and costume, with the work the actors have already created in the rehearsal room – and then to make the full effect as polished as possible.

Technical rehearsals can be very stop-and-start because if a cue doesn't go right you have to pause and correct the problem. So you rarely get to run a scene from beginning to end without stopping, never mind the whole play.

We are working with a revolve set which allows us to swap between several locations on stage without long, full changes of set between each scene. Being able to move quickly from one location to another is vital for this play as it helps us to build momentum and pace and keep the action of the play moving forward.

However, it also throws up many difficulties. Our set has been amazingly designed to provide three different locations, but as a result when actors are exiting a scene they have to be extremely careful that they don't walk

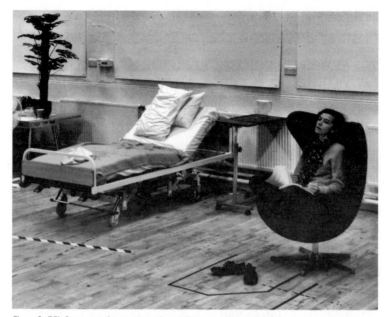

Sarah Vickers at home in the rehearsal room.
Photo © Dan Travis, deputy stage manager, Royal Lyceum Theatre

straight into the next scene. And when you're stood at the centre of a revolving set of doors it can be very hard to remember which door will lead you safely offstage and which will accidentally reveal you to the entire audience! This has led to much confusion and hilarity backstage with one actor often heard saying, 'I don't know where I am or where I'm going!'

A lot of our time during tech week has been spent working out how to perfect transitions between scenes. It is not just about the actors finally putting their performances onto the stage but also about the backstage crew being given time to rehearse their roles in making the play happen.

The stage management team have the tricky task of making sure each scene is set correctly, with all the right props and furnishings, without ever being seen onstage themselves as that would break the illusion of the world we are trying to create.

Due to the fast pace of the show there are also a number of lightning-quick wardrobe changes that the actors have to make. Sometimes with less than a minute between leaving a scene and appearing in the next scene in a totally different outfit.

Zoe and Jo, our assistant stage manager and dresser, spend most of the show hiding in various tiny corners of the revolve making sure that all this can happen, and occasionally having to push actors out of view of the audience when a door swings open at the wrong time. It's a mind-bending task that they're faced with and the show just wouldn't be able to work without them.

My role during tech week has mostly involved running up and down the three floors of the theatre's auditorium to check sight lines and ensure that all the action onstage can be seen and heard by the full audience – all 658 seats!

I've also been running lines with the actors whenever they're not needed onstage, standing in for them while lights and sound are plotted during breaks, and taking note of scenes we want to work on and feeding back ideas to the cast.

September 28th 2013
Previews: The last few steps on the Royal Lyceum's *Dark Road*

Previews are like the laboratory trial for a show. In a preview you recreate the conditions of the final production as closely as possible by having all the technical elements of the play in place and putting it in front of an audience.

And, just like in a dress rehearsal, it's important to note things that are working and things that aren't so you can address them the next day.

Ian Rankin
Photo © Dan Travis, deputy stage manager, Royal Lyceum Theatre

But a preview is not the finished article. You need the previews to teach you how an audience reacts to the play and what technical problems might occur so that you can then refine the production accordingly.

We have been lucky to have three preview performances before tonight's official opening and this has taught us so much.

On Wednesday, when we found that the finale of the play that had worked so well in the rehearsal room just wasn't getting the desired response from the audience, we were able to change it.

On Thursday we trialled our new ending and found it much better but still in need of tweaking.

And last night, on Friday, we were able to present a slightly altered version of our new ending that we are really happy with and the audience really responded to.

We've also cut scenes and reordered the play over the previews and this has been essential in giving us a play that tells the story we want the audience to see and takes them on the right kind of journey. Without previews we wouldn't have had the flexibility to change these things or the audience feedback to know what needed changing.

I've really enjoyed seeing how different audiences react to the show, and gathering feedback in the interval and at the end to see what people predict will happen and how satisfied they were with the story. The most gratifying thing of all has been watching from the back of the stalls as people jump out of their seats and scream and gasp in all the right places so we know we've hit the thriller mark.

Tonight's opening night will be a much needed chance to put on nice clothes and socialise after all the madness and changes of this week. But it's been totally worth it because we now have a show that we are all really proud of and excited to share, so all there is left to do is officially open it to the public!

Photo © Dan Travis, deputy stage manager, Royal Lyceum Theatre